DIVE
Like a Pro

by Robert N. Rossier

101 Ways to Improve
Your Scuba Skills
and Safety

BEST PUBLISHING COMPANY

ISBN: 0-941332-75-6
Library of Congress catalog card number: 98-83116

Composed, printed and bound in the United States of America.

Best Publishing Company
2355 North Steves Boulevard
P. O. Box 20100
Flagstaff, Arizona 86003-0100 USA

To Lori, Rachel and Ethan

Acknowledgements

So many people contributed to this book in so many ways, it would be impossible to thank them all. Special thanks are due to the fine folks at Dive Training magazine for publishing excerpts of the manuscript. I also wish to thank the staff at Diver's Alert Network (DAN) for many safety-related data and statistics quoted in these pages. The research done in preparation for numerous articles appearing in Dive Training and DAN's Alert Diver helped paved the way for this book as well. I also wish to thank all the divers, instructors, dive center owners, and friends who provided input at some level for the ideas presented in each chapter. Of course, I never would have attempted this project without the encouragement of Jim Joiner of Best Publishing.

Most importantly, I want to thank my wife Lori for helping me find the time and providing the constant encouragement needed to see the project through. Without her love and support, it would have been impossible.

Preface

It seems incredible to me that people can learn to dive in a weekend. Dive centers all around the country, perhaps all around the world, offer weekend versions of the basic open water certification course. Considering all there is to learn, an all the skills to be mastered, completing a basic scuba course in any format is an accomplishment of which any certified diver should be proud. Still, there's more to diving than can be learned in a weekend. In fact, diving is a life-long sport that demands continuing education at some level. No matter how much you know about diving, it seems there's always more to learn. And no matter how good a diver you become, it seems there is always some skill, technique or procedure that can be improved.

When I first learned to dive, I was lucky enough to have a group of experienced divers who became my mentors. They taught me the tricks of the trade and tips that made diving easier and safer. I probably learned as much from them as I did in my basic scuba course. Throughout my career as a dive journalist, I've had the opportunity to dive with scores of instructors and divers in an amazing spectrum of diving environments. It is my hope that this book, like my mentors, will help pass along the tips and tidbits that I've accumulated throughout the years.

This book doesn't have all the answers. But the information contained within its pages can help new divers climb the steep learning curve we all must negotiate at the beginning of our diving careers. Even highly experienced divers may learn or relearn a tidbit of information they never knew or happened to forget. And if you have any other good tips, be sure and let me know.

Contents

Acknowledgements v

Preface vi

1) Save Your Breath: 10 Ways to
   Safely Conserve Air 1

2) Hot Tips for Diving Cool Waters 11

3) Sink or Swim: Secrets to Better
   Buoyancy Control 19

4) Seven Ways to be a Better Buddy 29

5) Ten Ways to Build Confidence 37

6) Diving Fitness: Six Steps to Self Assessment 53

7) Ten Ways to Tune Your Gear 63

8) $ave Your Equipment: Tips on Care
   and Maintenence 71

9) Breathe Easy: How to Get a Good (and Safe)
   Air Fill 83

10) Ten Tips to Dodge the DCS Bullet 93

CHAPTER ONE

Save Your Breath: 10 Ways to Safely Conserve Air

1) **Stay Warm**

2) **Control Your Buoyancy**

3) **Avoid Sawtooth Profiles**

4) **Take it Easy**

5) **Streamline your Gear**

6) **Navigate Efficiently**

7) **Go With the Flow**

8) **Stop Those Leaks!**

9) **Avoid Air-Wasting Practices**

10) **Keep a Cool Head**

One mark of an experienced diver is low air consumption. While physiological factors such as body mass, work rate, and conditioning determine, in part, our breathing requirements, pound for pound and minute for minute, experienced divers typically use less air. What is it about experienced divers that makes them use less air? What black magic have they learned that is not taught to new divers?

While the ability to conserve air on a dive might seem like black magic, the secrets to low air consumption are really just common sense and simple science. The truth is, even new divers can master the art of conservative air consumption.

1 STAY WARM

Probably the most important key to air conservation is to stay warm. When we're cold, our metabolism increases in an effort to generate more body heat. It takes more air to fire the internal furnace, and consequently, our air consumption increases. By increasing our thermal protection, we minimize heat loss and the increased air consumption associated with higher metabolic rates.

Everybody has their own personal cold tolerance and threshold for comfort, but what many divers fail to realize is that comfort is a poor measure of our actual heat loss. Generally, a person feels warm as long as the skin temperature is around 85 degrees. In air, 85 degrees is fine, and we can run around scantily clad without feeling the slightest bit cool. In the water, 85 still feels good, but energy (heat) is transferred to the water at a rate of roughly 25 times that of air at the same temperature. In fact, a diver who stays in the water too long, can become dangerously cold (hypothermic) without even realizing there's a problem. So, as long as you don't feel too warm or uncomfortable in the water, consider adding an extra layer or piece of thermal protection.

It's important to keep warm not just while we're under water, but throughout the entire dive outing. We generally consider a surface interval between dives as a time to warm up, but it's easy to increase our cold exposure during the surface interval. Standing around in a wet exposure suit or bathing suit with a breeze blowing over your body, results in evaporative cooling that can sap the heat from your system. To minimize heat loss during the surface interval, consider changing into some dry clothes or don a dive parka that can be worn over a wet exposure suit.

2 CONTROL YOUR BUOYANCY

Instructors constantly harp on their students about proper buoyancy control. Beyond the fact that poor buoyancy control can be dangerous (and make us look inept) buoyancy control actually goes a long way toward minimizing air consumption.

Consider this: If you're slightly positive or negative, you must constantly kick with your feet or skull with your hands in order to maintain your depth. That's a lot of work, and although the extra work may help keep you warm in cold water, it's a waste of energy, and wasting metabolic energy means wasting air.

There's actually more to the buoyancy consideration than being neutrally buoyant. It's also important to be properly trimmed and correctly weighted. If your weight and buoyancy aren't positioned well around your body, you aren't properly trimmed; meaning you won't float in the right position in the water. A properly trimmed diver floats nearly horizontal, or slightly feet-up. If you're not trimmed correctly, you'll commit one of two air wasting acts. You'll kick your feet and skull your hands to stay in the proper position, or you'll swim through the water at an angle, which creates an enormous amount of swimming resistance or "hydrodynamic drag." Either way, you'll be working harder and breathing more air.

Carrying too much weight is a problem, even if you are neutrally buoyant. With too much weight on your belt, more air is required in your BC to compensate. The more your BC is inflated, the more drag it creates as you swim through the water. Increased drag means more energy spent kicking, and hence, higher air consumption.

Controlling buoyancy not only affects our air consumption, but several safety critical aspects of diving. To help get your buoyancy under control, refer to **Chapter 3**, Sink or Swim: Secrets of Better Buoyancy Control.

AVOID SAWTOOTH PROFILES

We all have our ups and downs in diving, but the sawtooth profile is a real air-burner. Every time we descend, we add a little bit of air to our BC in order to maintain neutral buoyancy. As we ascend, we vent that air from our BC. With enough up-down cycles in a dive, we can blow a lot of wasted air into the water.

Instead, plan your dives carefully, and strive for a relatively constant depth throughout the greater portion of the dive. If you're diving a new reef, wreck, or wall, make an initial survey at a relatively constant depth. It is much easier to then plan later dives to further explore features that lie at greater and lesser depths.

Not only is the sawtooth profile an air burner, it also predisposes us to decompression sickness. For more on this aspect, check out **Chapter 10: Ten Tips to Dodge the DCS Bullet.**

TAKE IT EASY

It's not a race down there, so unless there's a shark on your tail, take a leisurely pace to conserve energy and air. This one is a no-brainer when we consider some basic hydrodynamics. Water is about 800 times denser than air, so it takes a lot of energy to propel us through the water. Doubling our speed underwater requires four times the propulsive energy. To make matters worse, as we increase our metabolic rate to swim at a faster speed, we also struggle against increased breathing resistance from our regulator and decreased efficiency of our fins. If we double our speed (say from one knot to two knots), we might increase our breathing rate even more than four-fold. It's a losing battle, so relax and take a slow, leisurely pace.

5 STREAMLINE YOUR GEAR

Reducing drag, or streamlining, is another key element in air conservation. Cave divers are incredibly air-conscious, and these masters of the streamlining art go to great pains to minimize the drag of their equipment. We can take a few pointers from our subterranean diving counterparts to reduce our drag too.

The first step in streamlining is to stow those dangling gages. They create enough resistance just dragging through the water, never mind when they get pulled through the sand, silt, and mud, or get caught on coral reefs, rocks, and wrecks. Put clips on your computer and instrument console, and clip them to convenient D-rings on your BC (add one if there isn't one in a convenient location). The same goes for that octopus. Use a retainer to keep it out of harm's way and readily available.

When it comes to dive accessories, the rule is use it or lose it. Excess equipment only causes unnecessary drag, so if you don't need something, leave it behind. For a daytime dive, use a small dive light rather than that massive underwater torch that can light up the entire Gulf of Mexico. If you don't need your snorkel for a dive, consider removing it from your mask strap. A snorkel flapping around on your head is not only annoying, it wastes propulsive energy.

All equipment needed for a dive should be properly stowed. Put that underwater slate in your BC pocket and stow the fish identification chart and dive tables until you need them.

Picking the right equipment is also a part of the streamlining process. Instead of a large, high-volume mask, consider using a smaller one with a low drag profile. A low volume mask takes less air to equalize as well, so there's an additional attribute. The same goes for a BC. A small, streamlined BC with sufficient buoyancy for your needs will create less drag than a big, bulky device with enough reserve buoyancy to raise the Titanic.

In addition to being properly weighted, consider using drop weights to further streamline your profile at depth. A drop weight is nothing more than a weight with a clip that can be easily detached underwater. By removing some of your weight at depth (leave it clipped to the anchor line or an ascent line hanging from the boat), you minimize the amount of air carried in your BC, thus reducing your drag. At the end of the dive, clip the weight back on for the ascent and safety stop.

6 NAVIGATE EFFICIENTLY

Nothing wastes air more readily than getting lost under water. The time spent swimming in circles looking for a particular rock, wreck or reef under water is a complete waste of air, which reduces the time available for exploring, photographing, or whatever it is that you came to do. The same goes for getting back to the boat or shore. If you don't know where

you're going, you'll waste a lot of time and air just getting
there. If you have to ascend to the surface in the middle of
the dive to get a compass bearing, you've wasted even more
time and air. If you find yourself wasting time trying to find
your way underwater or getting back to the shore or boat,
take some time to brush up on your navigation skills. Work
with an instructor one on one or consider taking an underwater navigation specialty course at your local dive center.

GO WITH THE FLOW

A current or tide can be a blessing or a curse, depending on how
a dive is planned. To conserve energy and air, plan your dives
to take advantage of currents rather than struggle against them.
By planning a drift dive rather than returning to the starting
point, we can relax and let the current do most of the work for
the entire dive, instead of kicking against the current to return.

Since a drift dive isn't always an option, adopt a strategy of avoid-
ance whenever possible. A tide and pilot guide purchased at a
local marina will list the times for high and low tides and may also
provide important information on currents. This information can
help you plan your dives to avoid tidal flows and currents.

STOP THOSE LEAKS!

There's nothing worse than simply letting good air bubble
away needlessly. To reduce leaks, we can take another lesson
from cave divers. At the beginning of each dive, cave divers

perform a bubble check. Each buddy pair drops below the surface, and the divers take turns checking each other for air leaks. Small leaks may not seem like serious problems, but they do add up. Some leaks at the surface may become worse at depth, and a constant flow air leak at 66 feet will waste three times as much air as it does at the surface.

When performing a leak check, scrutinize everything. Look for leaks at all high and low pressure connections. Sometimes, all that's needed to stop a leak is to break and remake the connection. If that doesn't work and you don't have the tools or knowledge to fix the leaks yourself, have a professional dive center check out the problem.

Finally, avoid using a leaky mask. Each time you clear your mask, you waste time and air, so make sure your mask fits properly.

AVOID AIR-WASTING PRACTICES

It's surprising how much air some divers waste without giving it a second thought. A thorough evaluation of your personal

The Sniff-Check Fit Test
The best way to check the fit is with a suction test. Start by putting a snorkel or regulator mouthpiece in your mouth so your face assumes the shape it will have when diving. Flip the mask strap out of the way, hold the mask against your face, and inhale through your nose. The mask should stick to your face. If the suction is lost and the mask pops off, look for a better fitting model.

diving style and techniques can help identify and eliminate wasteful practices. For example, rather than wait for your buddy at the bottom of the anchor line, wait at the surface. While you wait, use your snorkel rather than breathing from your regulator. On the surface, don't fill your BC with the auto-inflator, use the oral inflator instead. A freeflowing regulator wastes a lot of air quickly, so make sure your octopus is positioned not to freeflow on the surface.

10   KEEP A COOL HEAD

Finally, remember that state of mind can affect your underwater performance, including your breathing rate. Any time we're nervous, our pulse and breathing rate become elevated. On the other hand, if we're comfortable in the water, our psychological stress is minimized along with our breathing rate. There are numerous ways of lowering stress levels in the water, but some of the most important ones are to dive frequently, take advanced or specialty training, and dive within your personal comfort zone. For more tips on building confidence, check out **Chapter 5**, Ten Ways to Build Confidence.

Lowering your air consumption not only allows you more time to enjoy the underwater world, it enhances safety as well. By returning from depth with more air left in your cylinder, you are better prepared to deal with an emergency or assist another diver. And you'll have the added satisfaction of looking and feeling like a more experienced diver.

CHAPTER TWO

Hot Tips for Diving Cool Waters

1) Get a Clue

2) Fuel the Internal Furnace

3) Dress Warmly Before and After the Dive

4) Choose Proper Exposure Protection

5) Keep Your Head Warm

6) Take Long Surface Intervals

7) Use Your Dive Log for Planning

8) Beware of Active Heaters

The need to keep warm on a dive isn't just a comfort issue, it's a safety issue, as well. Remember that being cold may increase the predisposure to DCS (see **Chapter 10**, Ten Tips to Dodge the DCS Bullet), and it increases air consumption (see **Chapter 1**, Save Your Breath). Being cold slows motor coordination, making it difficult to perform some tasks. It also affects judgment. The bottom line is that a cold diver is a dangerous diver, so here are some hot tips on how to keep warm on a dive.

1 GET A CLUE

The first step in keeping warm on a dive trip is to do your homework. Find out what the water and air temperatures will be, and plan accordingly. Be sure to factor in the possibility of cloudy weather, wind, and the fact that you may be wet even when you're on the surface. Also, take into account the number of dives you plan to make, since repetitive dives mean an increased need for thermal protection.

2 FUEL THE INTERNAL FURNACE

This may seem like common sense, but we must have energy to burn in order to stay warm. Head out with nothing but a cup of coffee under your belt, and your diving will suffer. To ensure you have enough fuel to burn for the day's activities, start by having a good meal before head-ing out. If you're planning to be out for several hours or to make repetitive dives, bring along something to eat between dives.

3 DRESS WARMLY BEFORE AND AFTER THE DIVE

Heat loss is an ongoing process. To stay warm, it's important to dress properly before, between, and after dives. The boat ride to the dive site can cause you to loose a significant amount of body heat before you even get in the water. Especially if you become wet with spray, the evaporative cooling can rob the body of precious energy and chill a diver to dangerous levels before he/she even makes his first dive.

On the way to the dive site, stay warm and dry. Instead of working on your tan, consider wearing long pants and a warmup jacket to retain as much heat as practicable. A cap or hat can also help reduce heat loss from the head, which can account for a considerable percentage of your total heat loss. Remember that even a mild breeze can increase heat loss, so consider wind chill when selecting travel attire (see Figure 1, Wind Chill Temperatures). On a sunny day, while diving tropical waters, resist the temptation to ride on the bow and frolic in the spray. Either wear a waterproof garment, or better yet, ride somewhere where you're protected from chilling wind and spray.

Divers often underestimate the heat loss that occurs between dives. Standing around in a wet bathing suit, dive skin, or wetsuit can result in major heat loss, as the evaporating water sucks the heat energy from out skin. To minimize the heat loss, change into something warm and dry between dives. As an alternative, get a dive parka designed to be worn over a wet exposure suit. These garments reduce the evaporative cooling, protect us from the wind, and add an important layer of insulation to limit the loss of body heat.

Even after our dives, it's important to tend to our body's thermal balance. Remember that rapid cooling or a depressed body temperature can alter our circulation and impede the transfer of gasses critical to preventing decompression illness (see **Chapter 10**, Ten Tips to Dodge the DCS Bullet). When the diving is done for the day, promptly get out of that wet gear and into some warm, dry clothing.   In the long run, you'll be glad you did.

CHOOSE PROPER EXPOSURE PROTECTION

What most divers don't realize is that comfort isn't the best measure of adequate thermal protection. Particularly at the beginning of a dive, we may feel quite comfortable, when in fact, the sea is silently robbing us of our precious body heat. Surprisingly, it is possible to become hypothermic when diving without proper thermal protection in waters as warm as 85° F. So how do we know what to wear underwater?

It's not always easy to decide what to wear on a dive. Wet suit or dry suit? Dive skin or a three-mil suit? Hood or no hood? How about mitts, gloves, or booties? Each of us has our own preferences and comfort levels, but a general rule is to wear a little bit more than what you think (or feel) you need. Particularly if you plan to make repetitive dive, it's easy to underestimate your thermal protection needs, and end up chilled during a subsequent dive. For those lacking the experience of diving in various climates, the following table provides some basic guidelines.

Table 1: Minimum Thermal Exposure Protection

Temperature	Suit Type	Thickness
Above 85°F/ 30°C	Dive Skin	single thickness
78–85°F/25–30°C	Skin or Wet Suit– shorty or jumpsuit	1/8" / 3 mm
70–78°F/21–25°C	Wet Suit–full length jumpsuit	3/16" /4–5 mm
55–70°F/13–21°C	Wet Suit–2 piece w/ booties, gloves and hood	1/4" / 6.5–7 mm
Below 55°F/ 13°C	Dry Suit w/ boots, gloves, hood, underwear	as required

 KEEP YOUR HEAD WARM

Many divers will not opt to wear a hood even when diving in moderately cool waters. After all, a hood is restrictive and uncomfortable. An ill-fitting hood can interfere with the seal on our mask, causing the mask to leak. Air can enter from the skirt of the mask, injecting an annoying bubble of air in the peak of the hood that fouls up our buoyancy and pulls our head up. Trapped air can make the hood act like an earplug, causing even more discomfort. It's really no surprise that hoods are frequently left on the surface in divers' gear bags.

On the other hand, if you've ever dove cold water without a hood, you might recognize the incapacitating pain, like a railroad spike being driven through your skull, which occurs when an unprotected head is immersed in water too cold for comfort. In fact, as much as 30 to 50 percent or more of our heat loss can occur through the unprotected head. Since proper oxygenation is critical to the proper functioning of the brain, blood flow to the head is not reduced like it is to other parts of the body in response to decreasing temperature. So, if you want to be comfortable on your next dive, get a proper fitting hood and wear it. If the top of the hood isn't vented to let unwanted air escape, slice through the material to make your own vent.

 TAKE LONG SURFACE INTERVALS

There's a limit to the amount of time we can spend underwater on any given day. Even when diving in relatively shallow water, the practical limit is probably less than three hours or so. With that point in mind, plan your dives to incorporate a nice long surface interval to allow your body to rewarm between dives. Plan a relaxing lunch. Drink of some (non-alcoholic) beverages to replenish the body fluids and stave off dehydration. Discuss your first dive, and carefully plan the next one. Check your gear over and make any necessary adjustments or repairs. Simply sit in the sun and enjoy life. Time taken between dives will not only make your dives more enjoyable, you'll be able to spend more time in the water on each dive as well.

Particularly when the water is cool, don't rush back into the water after the minimum surface interval. Take the time to thoroughly warm yourself before jumping back in.

 ## USE YOUR DIVE LOG FOR PLANNING

There's more to a logbook than recording underwater hours, depths, and visibility. Keep a careful record of the water temperature, what you were wearing, how active you were on the dive, and how comfortable you were. Be sure to include surface air temperature, sunshine, wind conditions, and other factors that affect your overall thermal balance for the entire dive outing. Finally, make particular note of your thermal comfort at the end of each dive, especially if you made repetitive dives. Then use this record to help select the items and accessories needed when planning a future dive.

 ## BEWARE OF ACTIVE HEATERS

A number of manufacturers produce active heaters designed for recreational divers. You'll hear claims made of how much these devices increase your comfort and extend dive times, but few divers realize that these devices can actually trick our bodies into losing more heat.

One way our bodies control heat loss is by controlling the flow of blood to the skin. Blood flowing through tiny capillaries near the body's surface acts like a radiator. By increasing the flow of blood in the skin, skin temperature is increased, and more heat energy is removed from the body. Decreasing the flow of blood to the capillaries has the opposite effect, and serves to conserve heat. This strategy works well on dry land, but water conducts heat about 25 times as fast as air, so even if the water temperature is a balmy 85 degrees F, heat loss in the water is significant. When we trick the body into thinking it is warm by applying heating pads to the skin, the body responds by increasing circulation to the skin which in turn increases heat loss. Our best bet is to wear a proper-fitting wet or dry suit with the proper level of thermal protection for the water conditions.

CHAPTER THREE

Sink or Swim: Secrets to Better Buoyancy Control

1) Plan Your Dive

2) Make a Surface Buoyancy Check

3) Adjust Your Trim

4) Use Clip Weights

5) Use Short Bursts to Inflate/Deflate Your BC

6) Control Breathing to Make Minor Adjustments

7) Choose the Right Mask

8) Adjust for Fresh or Salt Water

9) Log Buoyancy Data for Your Dives

Have you ever noticed how some divers seem to move through the water with the grace of a dolphin, while others flail about awkwardly? One diver glides over the reef while another kicks up a cloud of sediment and bumps into everything. The graceful diver ends his dive almost as rested as he started, while the awkward diver is nearly exhausted. The key to underwater grace is buoyancy, and while experience may improve our buoyancy control, a few tricks can chop years off the learning curve.

1 PLAN YOUR DIVE

The first step in controlling buoyancy is planning. Several factors determine the amount of weight needed to achieve the proper buoyancy. The first is the type of exposure suit and accessories worn. The more thermal protection worn, the more weight is need to counter its buoyancy. The second factor to take into account is the depth of the dive. Exposure suits become more compressed and therefore less buoyant with increasing depth, and so less weight is needed—at least while at the bottom. Later we'll talk about using clip weights to effectively control buoyancy over a range of depths. Once we have a plan for the dive, we can determine the proper amount of weight to carry.

2 MAKE A SURFACE BUOYANCY CHECK

You don't have to go very far to determine whether or not your buoyancy is set correctly. With an empty BC and medium breath of air, you should float at the surface at eye level. Another way to check buoyancy is to put on all your gear and go to the bottom of the pool (or protected open water site). For best results, perform this exercise at roughly 15 feet-the depth at which you will perform your safety stop. Remove your weight belt, hold onto the free end, and let the belt rest on the bottom. If your buoyancy is correct, the belt will just touch the bottom. Any weight resting on the bottom represents excess weight, which can be removed from your belt.

3 ADJUST YOUR TRIM

While neutral buoyancy is important, it isn't the whole story. Equally important is your trim—your head-up or head-down orientation in the water. Even if your buoyancy is right on, improper trim will cause a multitude of problems.

In general, the proper trim attitude is nearly horizontal or slightly feet up. This attitude reduces your frontal area and thus, minimizes the drag created as you swim through the water (see diagram). A slightly feet-up trim minimizes reef

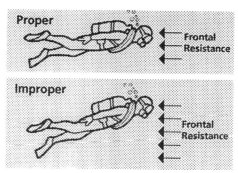

Proper

Frontal Resistance

Improper

Frontal Resistance

A diver in the proper trim attitude meets less resistance (drag) as he swims through the water than the diver who is trimmed improperly.

damage and reduces the potential for kicking up the bottom and reducing visibility.

To check your trim, take a medium breath and float motionless in the water in a horizontal position. If your feet tend to rise, try shifting your cylinder lower in the BC harness. If shifting the cylinder isn't enough, try a set of ankle weights and remove the same amount of weight from your weight belt.

If your feet sink, try shifting your cylinder to ride higher in the BC harness. You can also try removing weight from your belt and moving it to a BC pocket to shift the weight toward your head. If these adjustments aren't enough, try clip weights (see below) or a low volume mask.

4 USE CLIP WEIGHTS

Cave and wreck divers are sticklers for buoyancy and trim control. They have to be. They simply can't afford to be bumping into things and stirring up the silt and bottom sediment. One lesson we can learn from them is the use of clip weights. A clip weight is essentially a weight with an attached clip. Instead of wearing the weight on a conventional belt, the clip weight is clipped to a D-ring, where it can be easily removed and reattached. The D-ring can be on the weight belt, the BC, cylinder, or virtually anywhere else that makes sense, depending on the purpose of the clip weight.

There are two primarily uses for clip weights. The first is to adjust buoyancy for depth. Sure, we can carry enough weight to be neutrally buoyant as our cylinder runs low and we hang out at fifteen feet for a safety stop, but that means inflating our BC excessively at depth. Inflating the BC excessively has two disadvantages: increased drag and improper trim. The clip weight skates us around the problem by allowing us to remove some weight as we descend, and retrieve it on our way back up. The clip weight can be attached to a down line (ascent line), anchor line, cave or wreck entrance, or any other convenient location depending on the dive.

The second use of a clip weight is to adjust trim. By providing a convenient location to attach the clip weight, the necessary trim adjustments can be made. If your feet tend to sink, attach the clip weight in a location on the upper body. If your head sinks, wear the clip weight in a lower position.

5 USE SHORT BURSTS TO INFLATE/DEFLATE YOUR BC

They say patience is a virtue, and that goes double while making minor buoyancy changes. Picture this: you're descending toward the bottom at a fairly good clip, being careful to clear your ears as you go. Approaching the bottom, you stop kicking, and realize that you're so heavy that you keep sinking. Using your BC like a hand brake, you squeeze the auto-inflator, and the air rushes in. But you're still sinking, so you continue squeezing until your BC blows up like a beach ball. Finally the descent is arrested, but the next thing you know, you're headed back to the surface like a Polaris missile. What happened? You were overcontrolling.

Overshooting buoyancy control, either by adding or removing too much air at once from the BC, is a common mistake. Changing buoyancy "on the fly" as you change depth is also a tricky proposition and adds to the overcontrolling problem. This is because you rely on a buoyancy change to counter the momentum of your descent or ascent. In the example above, you needed a lot of excess buoyancy to arrest the rapid descent. Once the descent was stopped, the excess buoyancy accelerated you in the opposite direction. The same can happen on an ascent. If you suddenly realize that you're ascending too quickly, you may be tempted to dump all the air from your BC. Sure enough, this stops the ascent, but then you're too heavy, and back down you go.

The trick is to make small adjustments, and to make them more often. On the descent, add a quick burst of air to your BC every time you clear your ears. Making a more leisurely descent will also help, since it prevents you from trying to use your BC like a brake. On the ascent, make frequent adjustments, dumping small quantities of air from the BC as you go.

6   CONTROL BREATHING TO MAKE MINOR ADJUSTMENTS

We all know that breathing normally and continuously throughout a dive (particularly an ascent) is a cardinal rule for avoiding a lung overexpansion, but the way we breathe can also help control our buoyancy. Experienced divers know this trick, and use it to fine-tune their buoyancy as they swim.

Here's how it works:
Once our buoyancy is properly set, the depth of our breaths can be used to make minor changes or corrections. A bigger, deeper breath momentarily increases our buoyancy, allowing us to rise slightly. Likewise, exhaling or taking a shallow breath can make us momentarily negative.

Another way to control buoyancy is to adjust the depth of our breathing. A typical person uses only about one-third of his/her lung volume for normal breathing, so we can adjust our buoyancy by controlling the inflation level of our lungs. If we keep our lungs more inflated during the breathing cycle, or "breathe off the top," we are more buoyant and must carry more weight on our belt. Less experienced divers often do this subconsciously. If we "breathe off the bottom," or have our lungs inflated less during the breathing cycle, we are less buoyant, and thus can dive with less weight.

 CHOOSE THE RIGHT MASK

This is a simple concept, but few divers ever stop to think about it. The purpose of a mask is to provide an air space in front of our eyes and allow undistorted vision, but the size of that airspace directly affects our buoyancy and trim. A high volume mask adds more buoyancy, requiring us to carry more weight. It also tends to rotate us to an upright position. If you find that your feet are heavy and your neck hurts while diving, try switching to a low profile mask.

ADJUST FOR FRESH OR SALT WATER

Whether we dive in fresh or salt water has a direct bearing on the weight we'll need to carry. Freshwater is less dense, so we displace less mass of water, and need less weight to counter the buoyancy. The trick is knowing how much weight to add or subtract when changing between fresh and salt-water environments. If we knew the volume we occupy, it would be a relatively simple matter to calculate the buoyancy difference between salt and fresh water, and determine the corresponding weight requirement.

Unfortunately, that's not the real world. The best we can do is adjust our weight by a percentage. That percentage will vary from one person to another, depending on body type and equipment, but a rule of thumb will help put you in the ballpark. Going from fresh to salt, add about ten percent more weight to your belt. If you need twenty pounds of lead in freshwater, try twenty-two pounds for a salt-water dive, and adjust from there. Going from salt to fresh, remove about ten percent of the weight from your belt. If twenty pounds is neutral in salt water, try eighteen for a freshwater dive, and fine tune the weight from there.

LOG BUOYANCY DATA FOR YOUR DIVES

The first tip for buoyancy control was to plan your dive, and the more information you record in your dive log, the easier it will be to plan your next dive. For each dive, make a record of what you were wearing, the extra equipment you carried, how deep you dove, and how much weight you needed.

Divers often forget to take into account the cylinder they were wearing, and this can be a big mistake. Buoyancy characteristics of scuba cylinders vary significantly (see Table 2), so be sure to note the size (capacity), material and pressure of the cylinder you used. The next time you plan a dive, review your log to find dives at the same depth and water temperature. The recorded data will help you determine the proper thermal protection strategy and the amount (and placement) of weight you will need to achieve proper buoyancy and trim.

Precise buoyancy control is as much an art as a science. It takes practice and attention to detail to master buoyancy control, but understanding the subtleties is the first step in mastering the skill. Follow these tips, and before you know it, you'll be gliding above the reefs with the grace of a dolphin.

Table 2: Cylinder Specifications

Material	Capacity Cu. Ft.	Empty Weight Lbs	Working Pressure PSI	Buoyancy (lbs)* Empty/Full
Steel	71	29.5	2250	- 4.6 / -10.3
Steel	98	38	2640	0/-6.7
Steel	100	33	3500	0/-7.4
Steel	131	47	2640	0.8/-10.3
Aluminum	78.2	35	3000	2.3/-3.6
Aluminum	99.3	40.9	3000	3.1/-4.3

* Buoyancy figures are for salt water

Note: There are dozens of cylinders in service today. These specifications are only for a few of the more common ones.

CHAPTER FOUR

Seven Ways to Be a Better Buddy

1) **Know Your Buddy**

2) **Plan the Dive**

3) **Review Procedures**

4) **Assess Attitudes**

5) **Make a Pre-Dive Check**

6) **Keep in Touch**

7) **Stay Tuned**

One of the basic tenets of safe recreational diving is observance of the buddy system. We often forget is that buddies are a *team*. It's important for a buddy team to have a common set of objectives and to be tuned into one another. Throughout the dive, it's important to observe one another, and monitor each other's status. Regardless of your diving skills as individuals, your safety and performance as a buddy team will require you both to focus on being good buddies. If one of you isn't "into" being a buddy, you'll be little more than SOB's (Same Ocean Buddy's).

KNOW YOUR BUDDY

Your dive buddy is one of the most important resources you have on a dive, and knowing a few things about this individual can be vitally important to your mutual safety. It's good to know something about your buddy's diving experience, physical condition, equipment, diving style, objectives, and psychological state. If you're diving with a familiar buddy, you may already have a pretty good idea of his or her diving style and capabilities. You may be familiar with your buddy's equipment, and may even be able to assess his or her physical and psychological condition. Any time you find yourself with a new buddy, these factors can be the wild card in the safety equation. Through the process of reviewing the dive plan, suiting up, and performing an equipment check, you can begin to get to know your buddy.

2 PLAN THE DIVE

The dive plan should be squared away before you suit up. Be sure to review the key elements of the dive plan, such as the depth and time limits for the dive. These limits are particularly important when making repetitive dives. Also discuss navigation, who will lead underwater, and at what point you'll head back to the boat or beach.

Remember no two divers have the same skills or knowledge. Different divers use different types of equipment, have various eating and sleeping habits, and have different physical conditioning and stamina. Each of us has slightly interests and objectives. All of these variables should be factored into the dive plan (see Planning a Dive/The Seven Seas (C's).

Planning a Dive/The Seven Seas (C's)

Being dive buddies implies a fair amount of coordination and planning. One way to remember the key points in the planning process is to remember the Seven Seas (C's): Conditions, Cooperate, Coordinate, Cylinders, Compass, Communicate, and Check. Here's what to look for:

1. Conditions—Before a dive, assess all the pertinent conditions. Take into consideration sea conditions, visibility, lighting, temperature, surge, current, and any other physical factors. Assess your own physical and psychological condition (See **Chapter 6:** Six Steps to

Self-Assessment), as well as those of your buddy. If conditions aren't right, maybe it's a better day for bowling.

2. Cooperate—Diving is a give-and-take proposition, so be ready to negotiate on the objectives of the dive. Once you come to terms, you'll need to cooperate fully. For example, if you were planning on taking photos and your buddy wanted to spear fish, you may want to come to some sort of agreement or compromise. On the other hand, you might get some great shots of a shark attack.

3. Coordinate—One thing you'll want to agree upon is depth and time limits for the dive. If you're planning repetitive dives, it is especially important to set firm limits and stick with them.

4. Cylinders—As part of the planning process, compare notes on the size of your cylinders and your average air consumption. If you're a heavy breather wearing a 65-cubic foot cylinder, and your buddy who sucks the oxygen out of seawater is wearing a 100-cubic foot leviathan, you've got a serious mismatch. Consider switching to a larger cylinder, adding a pony bottle, or swapping cylinders with your buddy.

5. Compass—Regardless of the dive plan and objectives, it's always a good idea to decide who will lead once you get in the water. Remember, underwater wrestling matches are ugly, they waste air and attract sharks.

6. Communicate—Have you ever tried to give directions to a cab driver who didn't speak your language? The inability to communicate is frustrating in a cab, but it's downright dangerous under water. Before you hit the water, make sure you're using use the same hand signs as your buddy.

7. Check—Before you giant stride off the stern, be sure to have a plan for dealing with emergencies. This will require a thorough and complete pre-dive equipment check. Above all, make sure you know where your buddy's alternate air supply is, how to drop his weights, and how to inflate his BC.

3 REVIEW PROCEDURES

Even if you and your buddy hold C-cards from the same certification agency, you might not dive exactly the same way, so it's important to discuss procedures. For example, decide the depth at which you'll make a safety stop and how long you'll stay there. Review hand signals to make sure you're both using the same ones. Also review the procedures you'll follow in the event that you become separated under water.

4. ASSESS ATTITUDES

An important element in being a good buddy is learning to recognize and deal with different personalities. Some divers will make a better buddy for you than others, and the trick is learning to how make that assessment.

Throughout the pre-dive discussion, try to get a feel for your buddy's experience level, diving style, and attitude. Be on the lookout for any attitudes that may prove to be dangerous or incompatible with your own. For example, if you're inexperienced, you may not want to be paired up with a diver whose attitude seems to be, "I really don't need a buddy, but I'll let you come with me. Just don't slow me down." If you're an experienced diver, be cautious about a less experienced diver who may have an attitude of, "I have to keep up no matter what. I can't let my buddy down or look inept or inexperienced."

Some attitudes are potentially dangerous for any buddy. Statements like, "Oh, that's okay. This is a real easy dive anyway," may clue you into an attitude of complacency. Ones that sound like, "I really like making deep dives. Anything less than 100 feet isn't really diving," may signal a reckless attitude.

If you're not comfortable with your buddy, or if you feel your diving objectives are incompatible, consult the divemaster or instructor, and arrange for a different buddy. A bit of tact in this request can go a long way towards avoiding hostility and embarrassment.

5 MAKE A PRE-DIVE CHECK

Regardless of your plan, you can't be a good buddy unless you've completed a thorough pre-dive check. The pre-dive check is the last opportunity to evaluate your buddy's equipment as well as your own.

Different agencies and instructors teach slightly different procedures and may use different reminders for the pre-dive check. My personal favorite is "A Regular Buddy Often Gets Bent." The first letter of each word is a reminder of one of the key items in the pre-dive check: Air on and pressure checked; Regulator checked; BC checked (inflator and deflator); Octopus (or alternate air) checked; Gages (depth, bottom timer, computer, compass) checked; Belts and releases (weight belt, emergency weight drop releases) checked.

An alternate technique for making the pre-dive equipment check is the matching technique used by cave divers. One buddy leads, and the other(s) follows as the diver works from the top of the head to the feet, checking every single piece of gear on the way down, verifying that each buddy has the needed equipment and that it's functioning properly. This technique is very thorough and highly effective.

6 KEEP IN TOUCH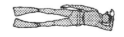

This is the first thing we learn in diving, and is often one of the first things forgotten: Always stay close enough that you can reach out and touch your buddy. If you can't touch your buddy, and rely on maintaining visual contact instead, you can easily end up as SOB's.

Losing contact with a dive buddy is a common occurrence, and it's more likely to occur when there's confusion about who is leading the dive. If it's unclear who is actually leading the dive, buddies are likely to become distracted and separated as one pauses to look at something and the other swims on. Buddies should be like a fighter pilot and wingman. The wingman flies just slightly behind and to the side of the leader, and it's the wingman's job to stay with the leader no matter what.

STAY TUNED

The most important thing is to stay tuned into your buddy. While you keep an eye on your depth, bottom time, and air pressure, keep an eye on your buddy's air pressure too. Look to see that your buddy doesn't have a dangling gage, loose cylinder, sagging weight belt, or other undetected problem. Stay tuned in by communicating frequently with hand signals, and watch his eyes for any signs of discomfort or distress. If anything out of the ordinary develops, resolve the problem or abort the dive.

Being a good buddy isn't easy. In fact, it's hard work. But the time and energy invested in being a good buddy and a good buddy team, pays high dividends in the form of safety.

CHAPTER FIVE

Ten Tips for Building Confidence

1) Take a Refresher Course

2) Plan the Dive and Dive the Plan

3) Fine-Tune Your Navigation Skills

4) Practice Safety Skills and Drills

5) Stay in Shape

6) Focus Your Underwater Vision

7) Take a Specialty or Advanced Course

8) Dive Frequently

9) Psyche Yourself Up

10) Know Your Limits

We like to think of diving as a physical sport, but in reality, diving is mental game of chicken. One of the most important keys to our safety underwater is our state-of-mind. If we have the confidence that comes with sharp skills and thorough knowledge, we fare well in the game. If we enter the water unprepared, our confidence quickly evaporates, and we find ourselves on a collision course with disaster.

Stress is a fact of everyday life, but too much stress can be a critical problem under water. The combined effects of physical, physiological, and psychological stress can quickly erode our sense of confidence and open the door to fear and panic. To help keep our confidence level at its peak, we must prepare ourselves both physically and mentally.

TAKE A REFRESHER COURSE

Like many sports and activities, scuba diving requires us to maintain a certain level of competency if it is to be done in a safe manner. Few skiers start the season by taking the chair lift up to their favorite double diamond mogul run. Common sense says it's a bad idea, so the wise skier starts the season on an easy trail to warm up and sharpen those rusty skills. Likewise, the wise diver starts off easy after a hiatus from the sport. Whether it's been six months or six years since you last dove, you're well advised to bone up on knowledge and polish up those critical safety skills before getting in over your head.

The amount and type of refresher training required, depends primarily on your total dive experience, recency of experience, and your personal confidence with knowledge areas and the water skills. If you've only been out of the water for a short while, a quick refresher may be all that's required. Get in the pool with an instructor, assistant instructor, or divemaster, and spend an hour or so reviewing basic skills like buoyancy control, fin pivots, mask clearing, and buddy breathing. A pool session or two and a review of the dive tables may be all you need.

If it's been more than a few months, you may need or want more than just a quick brush-up. If it's been a year or more, a full refresher may be in order. The scuba refresher (alias scuba review or scuba skills update) is designed to bring a diver back to a proficiency level necessary to safely dive open water. Typically, this includes not only in-water skills such as buoyancy control and mask clearing, but also a thorough knowledge review from dive tables to proper safety procedures.

A scuba refresher course can be thought of as a condensed version of the basic open water certification course. Expect four to six hours in the classroom reviewing everything from physics and physiology, to the use of equipment, and specific procedures such as proper ascent rates and continuous breathing. In some cases, a written evaluation is provided to ensure a thorough knowledge of the material. The pool session(s) provides an opportunity to assemble your equipment and complete a full skills review. The pool environment provides a relatively safe environment in which to scrape off the rust and regain a familiarity with the equipment in an underwater environment.

Most dive centers offer open water dives as part of the refresher program. Here again, you have the opportunity to ease back into the sport under the guidance of professionals. This is often the final element needed to reestablish a high level of confidence.

For divers with little experience and who have been out of diving for many years, a scuba refresher may not be adequate. If the refresher course isn't thorough enough, or if the pace seems too fast, consider retaking a complete open water certification course.

Is it Time for a Refresher?

Although most agencies recommend some type of refresher training after a break of six months to a year, there are no hard and fast rules. Remember that confidence is a major factor affecting your safety in the water, so if you think you might need a scuba refresher course, chances are you do. If you're uncertain, an honest assessment of the following questions may help you make the determination.

1) Has it been more than six months since my last dive?
2) Do I make less than 12 dives per year?
3) Do I feel confident with my open water skills and emergency drills?
4) Has it been more than three years since I was active in diving?
5) Will I be diving in a new environment or location?
6) Will I be diving with new or different equipment?
7) Do I have trouble calculating no-decompression limits for repetitive dives?

8) Do I have trouble calculating minimum surface
intervals for repetitive dives?

If you answered "yes" to any of the above questions, you
may want to follow up with some form of refresher
training at your local dive center.

2 PLAN THE DIVE AND DIVE THE PLAN

There's an old saying that previous planning prevents poor
performance, and it goes double for divers. By planning our
dives and sticking to that plan, we avoid many confidence-
crushing surprises. We should know where we're going, how
deep we'll go, and how long we'll stay. It's important to nail
down some of these parameters to ensure we don't overshoot
our NDL, especially for a repetitive dive. By having a good,
basic dive plan, we relieve some of the uncertainty and stress
associated with making a dive.

Following the dive plan is important, and the first step to
keeping a dive on track is to make a careful pre-dive safety
check. Equipment problems underwater can precipitate more
serious situations. A thorough pre-dive safety check will help
ensure that your gear will function properly during a dive,
and help prevent the need to make a change of plans mid-
dive to cope with an emergency.

Next, monitor your progress throughout the dive. The last
thing we need under water is a big surprise like running out

of air or exceeding our no-decompression limit. Make it a habit to closely monitor air pressure and bottom time. In addition, take stock of your physiological and psychological condition. If you become cold or tired, end your dive early.

Having a backup plan to deal with potential problems also reduces the stress should problems arise. In reality, some dives just don't go the way we plan. We end up going a little deeper, or not so deep. We find something of interest along the way and stop to investigate. We use more air than we expected, and have to cut our dive short. Maybe our buddy has an ear problem, and we must change our plan midstream. Any glitch in our dive plan can require some rapid replanning. If you've thought about that potential, have a backup plan, and know the dive tables, dealing with a change in the dive plan will be much less stressful.

3   FINE-TUNE YOUR NAVIGATION SKILLS

The underwater world is a beautiful one, but let's face it, it's foreign. We're aliens. We don't belong there. And as soon as we run low on air, we'll be leaving. At that point, we'd better know where to go to get "home." One of the most primal fears is that of getting lost or disoriented under water, so it only stands to reason that improving our navigation skills will help put our minds at ease.

One of the basic tenets of successful underwater navigation is a pre-dive review. The more we learn about the geography of our under water playground from an instructor, divemaster, fellow diver, or written guide; the better prepared we'll be to get around safely and confidently. So take the time, get a map, ask some questions, and be prepared.

The most basic piece of navigation equipment is the magnetic compass. If you don't know how it works or how to use it, you're at a distinct disadvantage. A basic underwater navigation course teaches the necessary skills and builds the confidence needed to navigate effectively underwater. If it's been a while since you've used your compass, practice a few navigation skills on land before you hit the water. The time spent refreshing your navigation knowledge can pay big dividends under water.

Navigation Tips

Underwater navigation does take practice to master, but there are some basic patterns that can help you get around under water. Using some basic compass techniques and timing, you can gage your position by following a predetermined pattern. As long as you avoid currents and maintain a fairly regular pace, the technique will work quite well and keep you oriented.

Several patterns can be followed using a compass and timing to help you maintain orientation. The simplest is the course reversal. Swim in a straight line for the first half of the dive, then turn around and swim in the opposite (reciprocal) direction for the second half of the dive. Another pattern I like to use is the triangular pattern. Start at the beach or boat, swim in a straight line for 15 minutes. Make a 60-degree turn (left or right), and swim another 15 minutes. Make one more 60-degree turn (same direction as the first one, please), and a 15 minute swim will bring you back roughly to where you started. The timing isn't critical as long as you keep a steady pace, and each leg of the dive is the same length of time.

Natural navigation techniques are also helpful on a dive. Following depth contour is a great way to make a dive, especially for a beach dive. Unless the bottom is an expansive flat area, following a contour will help you maintain orientation and find your way back to your starting point. Underwater landmarks make handy references as well, so keep your eyes peeled for easily recognizable features and make mental notes along the way.

 PRACTICE SAFETY SKILLS AND DRILLS

An important part of being confident in the water is proficiency in the basic skills and procedures of safe diving. If a flooded mask puts you over the edge, you really shouldn't be diving—yet. Go back to the pool, put on your gear, and spend an hour doing nothing but clearing your mask. The skill is mastered once you feel comfortable enough that you can clear your mask without even thinking about it.

The same goes for buoyancy control skills, and particularly the smooth and timely operation of the BC. One skill taught to divers is the fin pivot. This drill is usually practiced in shallow water. The objective is to set your buoyancy so that when lying motionless in the water, only your fins touch the bottom. Then by inhaling and exhaling, you pivot up and down as if doing pushups, with only your fins touching the bottom. It's a good skill as far as it goes, but it doesn't go quite far enough. Setting neutral buoyancy for a particular depth is one thing, but what is often more difficult is the skill needed to quickly adjust buoyancy when changing depth. If this is a problem for you, and the fin pivot skill doesn't help, check out **Chapter 3**, Sink or Swim: Secrets to Better Buoyancy Control.

One fear that can weigh heavily on the mind of a diver is knowing what to do in an emergency, and herein lies the essence of practicing emergency skills and drills. If we routinely practice emergency skills and drills, they become both routine and reflexive, and we're more likely to perform them correctly in a stressful situation.

Probably, the most important buddy skill is the air share drill. Here's the bottom line on this one: If you don't practice the air share drill, don't expect to be able to do it in an emergency. The air share drill is something that requires constant practice. It needs to be second nature if we're to complete the exercise with any degree of success in the high stress environment of a real out-of-air emergency.

When practicing the air share drill, you may find that your equipment needs some fine-tuning in order to accomplish the drill safely and comfortably (see **Chapter 7**, Ten Ways to Tune Your Gear). The short hoses found on most octopuses or alternate air sources are simply too short to effectively share air and swim. Often times, the mouthpiece is upside down, making it almost impossible for the recipient (the guy who's out of air and about to panic) to get the mouthpiece into his mouth. And, of course, if the alternate air source is not in an easily accessible location (and even if it is), the recipient may take the donor's regulator out of his mouth rather than search for the alternate air source.

Cave and cavern divers have the air-share drill all sewn up. They equip themselves with long hoses, so they can share air in trail (one diver behind the other, single file), and practice this drill before every single dive. For them, it is second nature, and an air share emergency is much less of a stressful event because of this constant training regimen.

Another important skill (actually, a procedure) for developing confidence is the buddy check. Knowing that you have all the right stuff, that your stuff is working, and that your buddy has the right stuff and his stuff is all working can help allay the fear associated with the initial entry into the underwater world. If you don't know how to do a thorough and proper buddy check (or even if you think you do), check out **Chapter 4**, Seven Ways to Be a Better Buddy.

Since low visibility or loss of visibility is such a big stressor for divers, simulating zero visibility is a great skill for building confidence. This is best done in the pool, where the environment can be closely controlled and the drill can be performed in shallow water. One way to do it, is to place a piece of aluminum foil either inside or over the mask to obstruct vision. The diver then swims along underwater and waits for a "trap" or simulated emergency. These can come in the form of an entanglement (another diver holding his cylinder or other piece of equipment), an air failure (someone shuts the diver's air off), or a gear malfunction (such as a lost fin or flooded mask). The diver has to keep his composure and resolve the problem without surfacing, and without removing his mask or the tin foil. Even twenty minutes of this drill can boost a diver's confidence tremendously, and help prepare him for a real emergency in open water.

5 STAY IN SHAPE

Over-exertion can lead to high stress and panic, and an out-of-shape diver will fatigue more quickly and easily. A diver in good physical condition can more readily cope with a demanding underwater situation, and is less apt to become overcome by exhaustion.

There are three types of fitness—flexibility, aerobic conditioning, and strength—and each type of fitness is essential to our overall health and diving safety. More importantly, the training to achieve each type of fitness is different. Stretching exercises help promote flexibility. Aerobic conditioning comes from exercises such as swimming or jogging. Strength comes from activities such as weight training.

Being fit in one area, such as aerobic fitness, doesn't mean that you're fit in the other areas. If you think you may be lacking in any of the three areas of fitness, consult a doctor or sports trainer. Find an exercise regimen that works for you, and then stick with it!

FOCUS YOUR UNDERWATER VISION

One out of every two divers suffers from imperfect vision. On the surface, precision-ground glasses or contact lenses restore our vision, and seeing clearly gives us the confidence we need to manage our jobs and daily routines. Without these lenses, the world is blurry, confusing, out of focus. Without clear vision, confidence is impaired. The same thing happens under water. Even the magnifying effect of underwater vision can't restore the sharp focus needed to see properly. If you can't see your gauges clearly, you could be in trouble and not even know it. If you can't see your buddy, you could both be in deep trouble. And, if you can't see the eagle ray or circling blacktip shark, you might as well be back on the boat.

The point is, you owe it to yourself to have good vision underwater, and it will help you maintain a high level of confidence. Several options are available for clear underwater vision. These include the use of contact lenses, a precision-ground face plate for your mask, or corrective lenses bonded to the inside of your face plate. The best option depends on a number of factors, including the frequency and type of diving you do, and your uncorrected vision. To help sort out the options, consult the professional at your local dive center.

TAKE A SPECIALTY OR ADVANCED COURSE

Another confidence-building strategy is to prepare ourselves in a way that limits the fear and panic-inducing stressors. Take, for example, a fear of sharks. Just the mention of sharks in the water can induce or heighten any diver's anxiety, but divers who participate in shark behavior courses and learn the true nature of these creatures, often transform their fear into a healthy respect.

Other specialty and advanced courses prepare us in different ways. For example, a cavern diving or wreck diving course can develop the ability to manage multiple tasks underwater, and help us avoid the stress that comes with high task loading. Virtually any advanced or specialty course will help us with our basic underwater skills, and build a higher level of knowledge and confidence.

 DIVE FREQUENTLY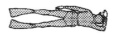

Diving skills, like any skills, tend to grow rusty unless we practice them. After a break from diving, you may find yourself forgetting the basics, or feeling awkward in the water. To keep a keen edge on your skills and confidence, participate in diving regularly. Although it might not compare in some ways to your latest exotic dive vacation, even an easy dive in a local pond or lake will keep your skills and knowledge fresh in your mind. Even a pool session at the local dive center can help keep you mind and skills sharp.

During periods when you simply can't dive, take the time to review the knowledge items associated with diving. Subscribe to a monthly diving magazine, and read it religiously. Review books or videotapes on diving. Even taking your dive gear out of the bag and checking it over will help keep you in tune with the sport, and help prevent that rust from accumulating.

9 PSYCHE YOURSELF UP

Diving really is a mental game, so it's important to prepare mentally before a dive. One technique we can use is visualization. If we rehearse the dive in our minds, we'll be more likely to perform well underwater. As part of the exercise, mentally review the steps you'll take in the event of an emergency, such as a lost buddy, regulator freeflow, or regulator failure. By having the steps boldly imprinted on your mind, you'll be better prepared to perform them in the water.

Although mentally rehearsing emergency procedures has benefits, try not to dwell too much on potential negative aspects of the dive. Focusing too much energy on the object of your fear, can raise your stress level, and narrow your perceptions. As psychologist Judy Lasher explains, "If you tell yourself, don't think of a zebra," you're immediately thinking about a zebra. You can't tell yourself not to think about something, not to experience something or not to do something, you have to tell yourself what you will do. Telling yourself, don't think about sharks." won't work. Your mind can only entertain one thought at a time, so that thought has to be positive, not one which focuses your thoughts on the object of your fear."

Back in the seventies, researcher and therapist Donald Meichenbaum, developed a series of techniques to help his patients cope with stressful situations. These procedures for mentally or rationally dealing with fear-producing stress may be helpful to divers. Among these, Meichenbaum would instruct his patients to:

a) assess the reality of the situation,
b) control negative, self-defeating, anxiety-arousing thoughts,
c) acknowledge the anxiety, and
d) psych themselves up to perform well.

An accurate assessment of a problem under water is critical to resolving it appropriately. For example, a free-flowing regulator still delivers air, so it shouldn't present a major problem as long as we're not in an overhead environment. The problem simply suggests that we signal our buddy, terminate the dive, and proceed to the surface.

Negative thoughts are seldom helpful in resolving a problem. Instead of focusing on the negative prospects of a problem, we do better to focus on the desired outcome, and take the steps necessary to achieve that success.

Acknowledging fear is healthy. Without fear, we might blindly dive to the depths of danger. We should remind ourselves that fear is both natural and positive, and use it as a tool to guide our planning, preparation, and execution of dives. By psyching ourselves up mentally, we are often better prepared to cope with the stressors which may accompany a dive.

10   KNOW YOUR LIMITS

Perhaps the best strategy for safe diving is to avoid the situations that can lead to panic. Regardless of the dive plan, always be sure to observe your personal limits. Any time we push the envelope, we put ourselves in a position where we can become over stressed and mentally lose control. Any time you don't feel up to par, refrain from diving. Don't push yourself to dive in excessively rough conditions, strong currents, or conditions of low visibility or strong surge. Avoid peer pressure, and keep your diving depths well within your experience and personal limits.

Divers are also urged to avoid environments they find uncomfortable. Although divers with claustrophobic tendencies may find that a mask with a translucent skirt will relieve some of the symptoms, they may still want to refrain from cave diving or wreck penetration. For those adversely affected by the sensations of high altitude, wall diving is something that should be eased into under the guidance of a professional instructor, or avoided altogether. Whatever our personal fears or limits are, we must be careful not to exceed them.

CHAPTER SIX

Diving Fitness: Six Steps to Self Assessment

Use the I'M SAFE checklist to assess your fitness for diving. I'M SAFE is an acronym which stands for:

1) **Illness**

2) **Medication**

3) **Stress**

4) **Alcohol**

5) **Fatigue**

6) **Eating (nutrition)**

One of the most difficult assessments we make as divers is assessing our physical, mental, and emotional fitness for a dive. Complicating the issue are various forms of self-denial which can suck us into unsafe diving situations just as surely as a whirlpool. Especially, when we go to great trouble and expense to go on a diving vacation, we can easily fool ourselves into believing we are fit for diving when, in fact, we are not.

Two critical assessments are needed prior to any dive. The first assessment is that of our personal skills and abilities. These can change year to year, or day to day, improving as we gain valuable experience and training. If unused, our skills degrade to where we are no longer capable of the same level of effort or degree of difficulty, that we could once safely accommodate. But our skills can easily change daily or even hour to hour as we experience various levels of stress and fatigue. The second assessment is that of the environment, and whether it is compatible with our skills and abilities at the time of the dive.

One tool to help assess fitness for diving is the I'M SAFE checklist. This six-step method of self-assessment was originally developed by the Federal Aviation Administration (FAA) as a self-assessment checklist for pilots. As you'll see, the checklist is equally valid for divers. In some respects, the assessment is even more important for divers than for pilots, especially when we consider the physiological impacts of the underwater environment on the human body.

I'M SAFE is really an acronym that stands for the six critical areas of self assessment—Illness, Medication, Stress, Alcohol, Fatigue, and Eating (nutrition). If we find ourselves deficient in any of these areas, we may want to reconsider our decision to dive, and put off diving until we can run through the checklist "clean." Here's what to look for.

1 ILLNESS

The first item on the personal fitness checklist is illness. Any sort of illness can be a potential problem, due to a reduction in alertness, reasoning, and reaction. But, some types of sickness also carry the potential for much more immediate physical dangers. For example, a head cold, congested sinuses, or chest congestion can result in squeezes, and other pressure related problems. Another type of illness common to divers is seasickness—motion sickness or mal de mare. This condition can leave a diver severely disabled, and unable to perform the physical and mental tasks required of diving.

Beyond the typical medical conditions like colds and congestion, divers must be aware that other medical problems are contrary to safe diving. For example, a tooth extraction and other forms of oral surgery can make it unwise to dive due to the risk of infection. Certainly, any other form of open wound can also pose a potential risk.

2 MEDICATION

Right on the heels of illness comes medication. Many divers take medication to relieve the seemingly minor symptoms of colds and other illnesses. With the symptoms gone, we may be lulled into a false sense of security, and deem ourselves fit for diving. Often, the reality of the situation is far from the case.

Medications, such as non-prescription pain relievers and cold remedies can cause secondary effects of impaired alertness and judgment. These same medications can also degrade vision, produce an upset stomach, and impair muscular coordination. Other medications, including non-prescription antihistamines, diarrhea medication, and motion sickness preparations can impair the same functions.

Anyone participating in a potentially dangerous physical activity such as driving a car, operating machinery, or diving, should be aware of manufacturer's warnings for numerous types of cold medications. For example, antihistamines can often produce drowsiness, dizziness, and blurred vision. Decongestants can also cause dizziness, along with palpitations, and excessive stimulation. Even appetite suppressants such as Acutrim and Dexatrim contain caffeine and other active ingredients that can cause dizziness, palpitations, and headaches.

While the side effects of these medications can be a problem on the surface, getting in the water and breathing compressed air while taking medication can be a whole different ball game. The effects of any medication, even non-prescription drugs, can be much different under pressure than in the one atmosphere environment for which it is intended. As Joel Dovenbarger of the Divers Alert Network (DAN) explains, "None of these medications were intended for use in diving, and there's no information available on the effects of using them in a diving environment. The combined effects of medication and increased nitrogen partial pressure can cause reactions, and may cause an amplification of the side effects. Often times the effects are subtle, but can lead to serious impairments. Reactions can vary from person to person, day to day, or even dive to dive." The message is clear. Diving with any type of medication adds an unknown degree of risk to the sport. In fact, non-prescription drug use was seen in roughly 20% of the diving accidents in 1992 alone, and prescription drug use was seen in roughly 30% of the cases that same year.

STRESS

Several types of stress can play an important role in a diver's personal safety. The various forms of physical and psychological stresses to which we are all subject on a daily basis, can have both beneficial and detrimental influences on our performance and under water safety.

Psychological stress can be that associated with the dive itself. Depending on your experience, and recency of your experience, you may harbor a certain amount of apprehension or anxiety relative to an upcoming dive. The uncertainties associated with diving in a new environment, or using new equipment or techniques, can also add to the level of psychological stress.

To a point, psychological stress associated with a dive can be beneficial. A low level of stress helps get our attention and focus our minds on the task. It helps us to remain uncomplacent. But too much of a good thing can cause problems, too. The effect of additional stress on a diver is a narrowing of perception. Psychologically stressed divers may be mentally preoccupied, resulting in decreased situational awareness. Taken to extreme, psychological stress can lead to panic, and complete loss of control.

Besides the psychological stress associated with a dive, we all carry with us a certain degree of emotional stress related to daily living. Normally, this stress poses no problems, but when our personal lives become complicated with issues such as marital problems, family illness, or job insecurity. When this happens, we can become preoccupied with these problems, and lose our ability to focus on less pressing problems.

Although these emotional stresses may be less a factor in diving than in some other activities, they are still worthy of consideration. We often think of vacation as a time to forget our cares and worries, but more often than not, they come along in trail. Concerns over work, family, relationships, or even travel in a foreign country can cause mental distractions, which can impair our decision making and judgment.

4 ALCOHOL

Diving, relaxation, and good times all seem to go together as divers head out on vacation or weekend underwater outings. Unfortunately, in today's culture, we also find a propensity for the consumption of alcohol during vacations and social outings, and it poses particular risks to divers. According to DAN, "The percentage of divers reporting alcohol use in dive accidents has remained constant for five years. The majority of alcohol use occurs primarily on the night before diving." The report goes on to state that at least one alcoholic beverage was consumed the night before diving in approximately 42% of all the 1992 accidents.

Alcohol affects us in a number of ways. One way is the decreased mental acuity and impaired judgment caused by alcohol consumption. Studies have shown that as little as one ounce of liquor, one bottle of beer, or four ounces of wine can degrade mental and motor skills, and will be evident in the breath and blood for a period of at least three hours. But, the effects go beyond those commonly associated with drinking.

Alcohol has other physiological effects that are of particular importance to divers. To begin with, alcohol is a diuretic—that is it causes us to urinate excessively—which can help lead to mild or even severe dehydration. Some studies have linked dehydration with an increase in the predisposition to decompression illness (see **Chapter 10**, Ten Tips to Dodge the DCS Bullet).

Alcohol also has a physiological effect on our heat balance. Alcohol is a vasodilator, which means that it causes blood vessels to dilate, or expand. This results in an excessive flow of blood to the skin and extremities, which produces a higher rate of heat loss. Divers who drink, are less comfortable in the water after a shorter exposure, and this reduction in thermal comfort may bring on additional physical and psychological stress.

The aviation world has long recognized the danger of mental and physical impairment by alcohol, and Federal Aviation Regulations restrict pilots from flying for a minimum period of eight hours after consuming alcohol. More recent regulations prevent pilots from flying with blood alcohol content of more than 0.04% by volume. Considering the potential dangers faced by divers who consume alcohol, perhaps similar precautions as those observed by pilots should be observed. In fact, with the potential predisposition to decompression sickness, divers might want to observe a waiting period before alcohol consumption following a dive as well.

5 FATIGUE

Another common risk which divers face is that of fatigue. In an effort to maximize the return on our diving dollar, it's easy to fall into the trap of doing too much diving, and wearing ourselves out. We all strive to get as much as we can out of our vacations, and divers often find themselves out enjoying the night life in tropical paradise, instead of catching the needed Z's to prepare for the physical demands of the following day's diving. While on vacations, divers are prone to push themselves to the limits of endurance, and although it may seem harmless, it can have potentially disastrous consequences.

There are two types of fatigue, acute (short-term) and chronic (long term). Acute fatigue is the tiredness you experience following long periods of physical or mental strain. Work, study, travel, lack of sleep, and participation in outdoor activities such as diving, can bring on episodes of acute fatigue. The symptoms of acute fatigue include reduced coordination and impaired alertness—both potential problems for divers. The cure? Adequate rest and sleep, regular exercise, and proper nutrition.

If we don't get enough rest between periods of acute fatigue, the condition can progress to chronic fatigue. This can be the end result of a dive vacation where we constantly push ourselves to enjoy both the diving and the nightlife. The result is a further degradation in physical performance. The mental condition degrades to the point where judgment becomes impaired to the extent that unwarranted risks may be taken.

It's not just our psychological state, mental acuity, or decision making that may suffer from fatigue. According to DAN, pre-dive fatigue or lack of sleep the night before diving has been consistently reported in about one third of all cases of decompression sickness in their database.

6 EATING

The final item on the self-assessment checklist is eating, or our nutritional fitness. Poor nutrition places additional stress on our bodies, and studies have shown a direct correlation between diet and mental acuity. Skipping meals or eating poorly before a dive may result in a decrease in our mental acuity, which similarly narrows our perceptions. In this state, we may be more likely to omit a critical predive check item, neglect to pay attention to our air supply during a dive, or improperly compute no decompression limits for repetitive dives.

COMBINING THE EFFECTS

The real problem comes when we start combining the effects of the above six fitness elements. Even minor deficiencies, when combined, can add up to major trouble, especially when a dive doesn't go as planned. Any time we're physically, mentally or emotionally compromised, our ability to cope with a minor equipment glitch or full-blown emergency can be seriously degraded.

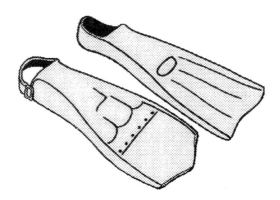

CHAPTER SEVEN

Ten Ways
to Tune
Your Gear

1) **Improve Your Exposure Suit**

2) **Add Clips and D-Rings**

3) **Make Your Alternate Air Accessible**

4) **Properly Position Your Guages**

5) **Streamline Your Gear**

6) **Use a Comfortable Mask Strap**

7) **Choose a Low Impact Weight Belt**

8) **Use a Custom Mouthpiece**

9) **Accessorize for Safety**

Modern dive equipment is a marvel of safety and reliability. Still, if you take a look at any experienced diver, you'll probably see a couple of non-standard additions to his complement of gear. No matter what equipment we're diving with, chances are there are ways to improve its utility and functionality. Here are a few tips for getting the most out of your dive equipment.

 IMPROVE YOUR EXPOSURE SUIT

Perhaps the most personal piece of dive equipment we use is our exposure suit, and there's nothing worse than using one that doesn't fit right. Over the past two decades, major improvements have been made on exposure suits. The materials are better, the suits more durable, and they fit better. Newer suits are cut properly to fit the diver's shape and motion. Even if it's custom tailored, the best-designed, most modern suit might not fit exactly right, or suit our needs (pardon the pun) entirely. So let's look at a few ways we can improve an exposure suit.

First, if your suit doesn't fit quite right, and purchasing a new one isn't in the budget, consider having it tailored. It's a relatively trivial matter to have modifications made to improve the fit. One sure sign of an ill-fitting suit is water movement within the suit. A spine or lumbar pad can be added to reduce water flow through these areas. Zippers or Velcro® closures can be added to the wrists and ankles to make donning easier and to provide a better seal. Material can be added or removed in other areas, in order to match the suit to your personal shape.

Another simple modification to improve serviceability, is the addition of kneepads. Depending on your style of diving, and the location where you dive, the knees of your suit can take a terrible beating. By adding pads, you can greatly extend the useful life of the suit. Finally, adding accessories such as pockets or new closures can add untold utility to your suit.

If your suit isn't quite warm enough, consider augmenting it with a new hood, chicken vest, boots, mitts, dive skin or undergarment. As with layering clothing on dry land, a layering concept for exposure suits allows a diver to more closely match thermal protection to the particular environment.

2 ADD CLIPS AND D-RINGS

As divers progress in the sport, take on new underwater tasks, and increase their complement of equipment, they often find they lack the necessary attachment points to secure their accessories. Adding straps, snaps, clips, and D-rings to strategic locations makes it easier to carry accessories and streamline their underwater profile. Clips and straps can easily be added to a BC to secure hoses, attach underwater lights, fasten communication slates, or photographic accessories. A metal band and D-ring attached to the scuba cylinder provides a readily accessible point to attach a line reel or other equipment. D-rings added to the BC, weight belt, or cylinder provide a convenient place to attach clip weights used for fine tuning buoyancy and trim.

3 MAKE YOUR ALTERNATE AIR ACCESSIBLE

One of the most prevalent common equipment problems seen under water is divers with inaccessible alternate air sources. Often times an octopus second stage simply dangles beneath the diver, dragging through the mud, sand, and silt. Other times, the regulator is secured within a BC pocket or other unseen location. More often than not, the hoses provided on alternate air sources are of insufficient length to readily accommodate a distressed diver. These problems are easily remedied.

Most instructors agree that the best place for an alternate air regulator to be positioned is on the divers chest, where it is readily seen and quickly put to use. Custom straps and fittings for attaching the regulator in this location are readily available at many dive centers, or can easily be made from a length of surgical tube and a couple of nylon tie-wraps. The length of tubing should be adequate to be easily worn around the neck, with the loose ends overlapped to form a smaller loop through which the mouthpiece of the second stage can be secured.

Making an ascent while air sharing can be exceedingly difficult if the hose connecting the second and first stages is too short. Cave divers learned this a long time ago, and typically equip their alternate air regulator with a seven to nine-foot intermediate pressure hose. These hoses are readily available through professional dive centers around the world. To keep the extra length of hose out of the way when not in use, they often coil the excess hose and slip it under a rubber (surgical tube) band placed around their scuba cylinder. This arrangement keeps the equipment secured and out of the way, while making it totally accessible in an emergency.

PROPERLY POSITION YOUR GAUGES

Another common problem that requires some fine-tuning is the placement of the instrument console or dive gauges. It's all too common to see divers swimming along the reef with their instrument console banging along the coral below them. This is particularly destructive to the reef, and it's a sure bet the diver has no idea of his remaining air supply or bottom time. Again, the fix is simple, and can be accomplished in any one of several ways. One fix is to attach a clip to the console that can be secured to a D-ring on the front of the BC. Some divers prefer using separate wrist mounted gauges, or attaching their console to their wrist.

STREAMLINE YOUR GEAR

This is something you hear often in cave diving and wreck diving circles, but it really has application in all forms of sport diving. Streamlining your gear is the process of properly securing all your gear and eliminating entanglement hazards. If you've taken the advice given so far, you're part way through the process of streamlining your gear, but there are a few more things that will help complete the process. In addition to securing that dangling console and properly positioning your alternate air supply, look for anything which can become entangled on a strand of monofilament fishing line or protruding portion of the natural or manmade marine environment.

Cave divers are fanatical about streamlining. They secure loose ends of mask and fin straps with layers of duct tape. Snorkels and other unnecessary equipment are removed entirely, or stored in a pocket. Another trick is to remove your knife sheath from your leg and attach it to your upper arm or the corrugated inflator hose for your BC. This makes swimming easier (you don't have that weight on your ankle or calf), eliminates a potential entanglement hazard (the knife handle protruding from your leg), and puts the knife where it can be easily reached, regardless of how you become entangled.

USE A COMFORTABLE MASK STRAP

Sometimes it's the little things that make life enjoyable, and having a comfortable mask strap is just one of those little things. If you've ever had a mask strap become tangled in your hair, or had one constantly slip out of position on your head, then you know what I'm talking about. The next time you visit your local dive center, check out the after-market straps. I like the big cushy ones made of neoprene rubber. They slide on and off with ease, yet remain secure without tangling things up.

CHOOSE A LOW IMPACT WEIGHT BELT

If you're like most divers, you probably spent a significant chunk of change on your exposure suit, and you hate to see it torn up by the rough lead weights that are found in resort rental service. Manufacturers now produce a myriad of low impact dive weights, including "soft" weight belts, molded weights, coated weights, and various clip weights.

Even if you don't want to carry your own weights with you (let's face it, you have enough to bring along on a dive vacation without lugging along lead weights), there are options which can prevent the suit damage. For example, a pocket belt has pockets into which conventional lead weights (or shot) can be placed. These make it convenient to adjust your weight, and eliminate the exposure suit damage. Yet another option is to use a BC with integrated weights. These often utilize weight pockets into which the rental weights (of virtually any configuration) can be added.

USE A CUSTOM MOUTHPIECE

Another complaint often voiced by divers is the discomfort associated with their regulator mouthpiece. Not all mouthpieces are alike, and a host of custom shapes and sizes, including moldable designs, are available to relieve the jaw fatigue and pain. Swapping a standard mouthpiece for a custom model takes about thirty seconds. Simply snip the old nylon tie-wrap, pull off the mouthpiece, slide on the new mouthpiece, and secure it with a new tie-wrap. Even if you're renting a regulator, a small stash of nylon tie wraps in your gear bag will ensure a comfortable regulator.

9 ACCESSORIZE FOR SAFETY

Numerous accessories are available today that add an increased level of safety to our diving. The accessories to consider depend primarily on the style of diving you prefer, and the locations where you typically dive.

Nothing is more important on a dive than breathable air, so regardless of the type of diving you do, consider the options for alternate air. A Spare Air (TM) or pony bottle and spare regulator may add a significant margin of safety, especially if your diving is taking you to greater depths or more demanding dive situations.

Getting help when you need it is also a primary safety concern, so consider some sort of signaling equipment. Signaling equipment such as a Dive Alert (TM), strobe, or flare can summon help and ensure you don't get left behind at the dive site.

Every diver should carry a first aid kit, and if you find yourself taking trips to more remote dive areas, consider enhancing the contents of the kit. Remember that the contents of a first aid kit should change, just as the contents of your gear bag changes. The further you'll be from immediate medical care, the more you'll want to have on hand for emergencies. Remember too, that first aid training and equipment go hand in hand. The more first aid equipment you carry, the more training is required to use it properly.

$ave Your Equipment: Tips on Care and Maintenance

Scuba diving can be an expensive sport, especially if we fail to give our equipment the TLC it deserves. In this chapter, we'll review some basic care and preventative maintenance tips for the following:

1) **Mask, Fins, and Snorkel**

2) **Exposure Suits and Accessories**

3) **Regulators**

4) **Guages**

5) **Buoyancy Compensators**

6) **Dive Accessories**

7) **Dive Computers**

8) **Equipment Bags**

Scuba diving is an equipment intensive sport, and a quick check of price tags in your local dive center will point out the importance of protecting that investment. Just a little extra care goes a long way towards saving your equipment.

If you're taking a dive trip to some exotic (or even not that exotic) locale, you'll have a lot riding on your equipment's condition. Before you pack up, take a few minutes to check your equipment and complete any required maintenance. Minor problems detected before a dive trip can often be resolved quickly and inexpensively, before they develop into bigger problems under water. Without the attention your equipment deserves, your next dive trip could be more expensive than expected.

Whether you're planning a dive trip, have just returned for one, or you're packing it up for the season, get out that gear bag and follow along as we review the basics.

 MASK, FINS, and SNORKEL

The most basic of all diving equipment is the mask, fins, and snorkel, and considering their importance on each and every dive, they deserve at least a cursory inspection before packing for a trip. An ill-fitting or leaky mask can make diving even the best locale a miserable experience, so put it on and test for leaks by inhaling. If equipped with a purge valve, hold the mask to your face and exhale to check the operation of the valve. Also check the skirt for minor rips, tears, or nicks, which may leak or deteriorate further. Rather than risk a problem on an expensive dive outing, replace an aging or ill-fitting mask.

Straps, especially those made of rubber, should be checked before every dive. A broken mask or fin strap can be a major show stopper, so make sure the straps don't show any signs of aging such as checking or crazing. Replace any suspect straps, rather than risk a problem under water. Bent or cracked buckles can also fail at any time, so replace those as well. Finally, to avoid a broken faceplate, pack your mask in a rigid storage box when traveling.

Nothing seems as simple as a snorkel, but even it requires some routine maintenance. Most importantly, make sure the mouthpiece is securely attached. If the bite tabs are damaged from overuse, either replace the mouthpiece or get a new snorkel. Also, replacing a worn or damaged snorkel keeper can save you from buying a new snorkel.

After a saltwater dive, be sure to rinse your mask, fins, and snorkel with fresh water. Take a couple extra minutes to dis-assemble, inspect, and clean the snorkel's swivel joint (if it has one) to remove sand and sediment. For long term storage, make sure all the equipment is thoroughly dry, and store the items in a cool, dry environment, out of direct sunlight.

2 EXPOSURE SUITS AND ACCESSORIES

There's no magic to taking care of a wet suit and accessories, but a little bit of common sense goes a long way. Rule number one is to keep wet suits clean and dry when not in use. After diving, rinse that suit thoroughly in freshwater. Washing with wetsuit shampoo will help remove oils, dirt and salt, and keep your suit smelling fresh. Hang the suit on a wide hangar to avoid damaging the material, and allow it to dry thoroughly. Most dive centers sell special hangers designed for wetsuits. Always hang a wetsuit in a cool, dry location for long term storage.

Before the start of the season, check the suit for excessive wear or damage, and inspect the stitching. Loose threads can be burned off to prevent unraveling. Major suit problems should be referred to your dive center, and remedied before your next dive outing.

Dry suit maintenance follows the same protocol as wet suits, but with a few additional details. Apply zipper lubricant regularly to keep the zipper moving smoothly. Also check the condition of the seals, and use talcum powder before donning the suit. Again, always make sure your drysuit is dry before storing it in the bag. Any dampness will encourage the growth of mold and mildew.

3 REGULATORS

Although modern regulators are highly dependable, a few minutes of preventative maintenance before and after each dive will help ensure reliability at depth. Before packing for a dive trip, give your regulator a quick "once over" for any obvious problems. Mouthpieces should be securely attached to the second stages, and make certain the bite tabs haven't been bitten through. Replace damaged mouthpieces before diving. If your jaws become tired while diving, consider installing a custom mouthpiece. Your professional dive center can show you the options available.

Following a dive, make a note of how your regulator performed. Any leaks, freeflow, or difficulty inhaling is a sure sign that professional maintenance is overdue. Water in the regulator first stage can lead to serious trouble, so always wipe or blow dry the first stage dust cap and install it immediately after removing the regulator from the cylinder. As you remove the regulator, check the first stage inlet filter for any discoloration that might indicate a developing problem.

Reading Your Regulator's Filter

The filter at the inlet of your regulator's first stage is designed to prevent foreign objects from entering the mechanism and creating havoc with your air supply. Monitoring this filter is one way of keeping tabs on your regulator's health. Discoloration of the filter is usually a sign of trouble down the road. If any of the following are detected, have your regulator checked out by professionals.

✓ Turquoise, green or white chalky residue is a sign that seawater has entered the first stage, and where water goes, corrosion and trouble follows.

✓ A reddish brown residue usually means tank corrosion, and the tiny rust particles can damage O-rings and precision machined internal parts.

✓ Black particles usually indicate a problem with the air station's compressor. Let them know about the problem, or consider having your cylinder filled elsewhere.

As with most scuba equipment used in seawater, a thorough rinse in freshwater is essential to prevent corrosion and the damaging effects of salt crystallization. Even if you dive in freshwater, a freshwater rinse (no chlorine please) will help flush out and remove silt, sand and other contaminants which may find their way into your equipment. However, a couple caveats apply to rinsing the regulator.

First, never push the purge valve when rinsing the regulator, as this allows water to enter the regulator. After removing your regulator from the freshwater rinse, be sure to shake the water out of the second stage. Water left sitting in the second stage becomes a breeding ground for algae and every other aquatic biocontaminant.

When it comes to long term regulator storage, the usual precautions apply. Store the regulator in a clean, dry, and cool area. If you use an expensive or custom mouthpiece, consider removing it for long term storage to prevent any deformities or damage. In addition to these preventative maintenance tips, regulators should also receive annual routine servicing, maintenance, and adjustments from a professional dive center. If you plan on ice diving, have that annual servicing done before the beginning of the winter diving season.

4 GUAGES

When taking care of your regulator, don't overlook the gage console. A freshwater rinse is usually all it requires, but a quick function test can help avoid problems underwater. Be sure your depth guage reads properly at the surface. Erroneous surface readings can translate to improper depth readings, so refer any problems to your dive center to verify the calibration.

The compass should be full of fluid (a few small bubbles are generally okay), and the needle should swing freely. Rinse the compass with freshwater to remove sand and salt crystals that can bind the bezel. Leaking or missing fluids and sticking needles mean it's time to visit the shop.

5 BUOYANCY COMPENSATORS

Most divers understand the importance of rinsing the exterior of their BC, but the bladder and internal workings require a thorough rinsing as well. BC's often have more valves and moving parts than a regulator, and a thorough cleaning is essential to ensure the mechanisms will perform as designed.

Rule number one is not to let your BC dry before it has been cleaned. Salt crystals, which form when seawater dries, can damage the materials and components. Either rinse the BC right away, or keep it in a wet bag until you're ready to do a proper clean-up.

Different manufacturers have different procedures for flushing out their BC, so read the instructions. One way is to remove the dump valve located on the shoulder, and the one located on the lower portion of the device. This provides large openings through which to flush out any large debris, sand and sediment that may have entered the bladder. Simply flush water through the bladder using a garden hose.

The oral inflator/deflator mechanism should only be flushed from the mouthpiece end. Emptying the bladder through the deflator mechanism can cause debris and contaminants to become caught in the spring mechanism and jam the valve.

Regardless of how you flush your BC, be certain to only use low pressure freshwater, not a high pressure spray nozzle. An occasional cleaning with one of the many chemical BC cleaners/deodorizers will help prevent algae from growing in the bladder and keep the bladder soft and flexible. When reassembling the BC, install all the rubber gaskets correctly, and be careful not to cross thread the valve assemblies as you reattach them.

For long term storage, start with a chemical rinse and conditioning, and remove the upper inflator for storage so the bladder can breathe. At the beginning and end of the season, give the BC a thorough visual inspection and check all the material, straps, and stitching.

It's a good idea to inflate the BC until it's stiff to make sure there are no leaks. If the BC doesn't stay firm for at least four hours, the problem may be a leaking valve or a pinhole leak in the bladder, so have the device professionally serviced.

It's a good idea to check the security of the low-pressure inflator mechanism. A missing tie-wrap can allow the inflator mechanism to pop off the inflator hose, rendering the BC inoperable. Also check the operation of the inflator and deflator valves. A sticking valve could lead to a runaway or inoperative inflator or failed dump valve, either of which could be a major problem underwater. Again, a professional dive center can perform the required servicing.

Even if your BC appears to be in good shape, it still should receive periodic professional maintenance. As with a regulator, annual professional maintenance of your BC will ensure proper operation and a long service life, and may be required to validate the warranty.

 **DIVE ACCESSORIES**

Now that we've got the major items covered, let's take a look at the accessories, such as dive lights, knives, and equipment bags. Dive lights usually require only a rinse in freshwater, but between dive trips, take care of the preventative maintenance. Any time you open the light, clean the O-ring, inspect it for damage, and lightly lubricate it with silicone grease. If any water has entered the light, dry the case out thoroughly and remove any corrosion that may have formed on the contacts.

For long term storage, remove batteries from the light. Then recharge or replace the batteries before each dive trip. Also check the operation of the switch, and periodically inspect the straps and lanyards.

A dive knife should always be rinsed with freshwater and dried before putting it away. A light coating of silicone spray will help prevent corrosion from occurring. Before a dive trip, remove any corrosion and sharpen the blade if necessary. Consult your professional dive center for the best products and proper techniques to clean and sharpen the blade. Check the sheath and replace worn or damaged straps and buckles.

DIVE COMPUTERS

Always follow the manufacturer's instructions for cleaning and testing your dive computer. Scheduled or periodic maintenance may be required not only for your own safety, but to keep the warranty validated. Battery replacement and other recommended periodic maintenance should be completed before the start of the diving season.

8 EQUIPMENT BAGS

Your dive equipment is no more secure than your equipment bag, so make sure it's in good condition. Broken straps, damaged zippers and excessive wear mean it's time to repair or replace your bag. After a dive trip, empty the bag, remove all the sand and debris, and wash the bag with wet suit shampoo or other gentle cleaner. Let the bag dry completely before repacking your equipment.

Although much of our dive equipment requires professional periodic maintenance, there's still plenty of preventative maintenance, inspection and servicing we can do ourselves. If uncomfortable with certain aspects of scuba equipment inspection and maintenance, consider taking an equipment specialty course. Although the course won't make you a certified repair technician, it does teach the rudiments of inspection, disassembly, and minor equipment repairs and adjustments. Proper maintenance not only protects our investments in dive equipment, but it's a great insurance policy for safe diving.

Stocking Your Save-A-Dive Kit

Periodic maintenance of our dive equipment is essential to safe and trouble-free diving, but even with the best of care, trouble can crop up at any time. A well-stocked Save-A-Dive Kit can mean the difference between soaking up the rays on the beach or deck, and swimming with the rays in the deep blue. Consider the following:

✓ STRAPS—Replacement straps for your mask and fins are the most basic ingredients of any Save-A-Dive Kit.

Many masks and fins require specialized straps, so be sure to carry the ones that fit your equipment, not a generic strap that may or may not fit.

✓ MOUTHPIECE—Regulator and snorkel mouthpieces often need replacement as the materials fails or the bite tabs are bitten through. A spare mouthpiece and tie-wraps make replacement a simple matter.

✓ O-RINGS—Be sure to include a few tank valve O-rings, as these often require replacement. Include spare O-rings for accessories such as dive lights or underwater camera housings as well.

✓ LUBRICANTS—Be sure to carry an assortment of lubricants in your kit. Silicone grease, silicone spray, and zipper lubricant top the list.

✓ BATTERIES—Power failures often plague the unprepared diver, so include spare batteries for dive lights, computers, strobes, and other accessories.

✓ BULBS—Batteries aren't the only reason why dive lights fail, so pack a spare bulb or two in your kit.

✓ TOOLS—Carry a few tools to handle minor equipment repairs. Include a few common size open-end wrenches, screwdrivers, allen wrenches, pliers, and knife. Many divers carry a Swiss Army knife, Scuba Tool, or Leatherman, which incorporate several tools in one.

CHAPTER NINE

Breathe Easy: How to Get A Good (and safe) Air Fill

1) VIP Regularly

2) Hydro for Your Health

3) Never Empty the Cylinder

4) Use a Dry Fill Hose

5) Watch Where You Fill

6) Check the Records

7) Test for Carbon Monoxide

8) Verify Nitrox Fills

9) Store Cylinders Properly

Divers are always concerned about getting a good air fill. After all, the charge of air in our cylinder determines in part the length of our underwater sojourn. Considering the money spent on training, equipment, and travel to a dive location, we hate to think of losing a minute's time underwater because someone gave us a bad (low pressure) air fill.

We also like to complain about the cost of air fills. After all, air is air, and it ought to be free. Instead, we pay handsomely to have it compressed into our cylinders. After a few dozen dives or so, any excess spent on air fills adds up to a shinny penny, and we'd rather spend that money on our next dive vacation.

If we look at air fills this way, we really miss the boat. We're focusing on the wrong factors entirely. The more we learn about air fills and air quality, the more we appreciate the unbelievable deal we get when we pay a few dollars for an air fill. The more we dive, the more we realize that our own habits and techniques influence the length of time we spend under water much more than an extra hundred pounds of pressure one way or the other (see **Chapter 1**, Save Your Breath). The more we think about it, the more we appreciate that there's more to a good air fill than pressure, and the more we're willing to spend on a quality air fill. When we consider the cost of training, equipment, and traveling across the globe to dive, the cost of an individual air fill is really insignificant, certainly less important than getting the safe, quality air that enables us to dive another day. So with these points in mind, let's take a look at how we can get the most for our money, and get a good, safe air fill.

1 VIP REGULARLY

The first defense in the guard against bad air fills is a visual inspection program (VIP). Designed as a safeguard for air stations against the hazards of cylinder failure, the VIP program also serves to protect the diver's investment by detecting problems before they get out of hand. In addition, a proper visual inspection will detect contaminants in a cylinder that may lead to reduced oxygen levels and other potential health problems.

While visual inspections are typically required on an annual basis, cylinders used in resort rental programs or frequently filled on boats or in humid areas should be visually inspected as frequently as every 3 to 6 months.

2 HYDRO FOR YOUR HEALTH

The second defense in the war against unsafe air fills is the hydrostatic inspection. Required every five years, the purpose of the hydrostatic test is to verify the structural integrity of the cylinder by subjecting it to pressures in excess of the normal operating pressure and measuring its expansion characteristics. Especially if there's a possibility that you might have damaged your cylinder, you'll want to have it hydroed before getting your next air fill.

A steel 72 filled to 2,000 psi has roughly the same potential energy as a Cadillac careening into a brick wall at 500 miles an hour. Should a cylinder fail due to neglect or misuse, it's sure to wreak havoc. With this in mind, resist the temptation to have your cylinder overfilled. Overfilling can weaken the cylinder, and lead to problems down the road.

3 NEVER EMPTY THE CYLINDER

Well, almost never. All divers are taught never to empty their cylinder completely on a dive. There are several reasons for this. First and most importantly, it's always a good idea to leave some air in your cylinder for emergencies. You never know when it might be necessary to take a few hits from your regulator while trying to negotiate heavy surf at the end of a beach dive, or when trying to get back on a dive boat in rough conditions. The other reason given is that when a cylinder is empty, water can enter and cause corrosion. Probably more likely is the potential for getting water into the first stage of your regulator when the purge button is accidentally pushed on the second stage. In any event, it's a good idea to leave some pressure in the cylinder.

Some divers scream at the thought of having to empty their cylinders to have them flown on an aircraft. Unfortunately, scuba cylinders are considered "hazardous materials" and require special handling by airlines. Depending on the airline, the aircraft in question, and the facilities for storing the cylinder on the aircraft, you may be required to open the cylinder and relieve all the pressure. If you're concerned about contaminants entering your cylinder under these circumstances, simply put some tape over the inlet to prevent anything from entering. In reality, there's little to worry about in terms of contamination entering your cylinder on an airplane ride. You're much more likely to have contamination enter your cylinder the next time you get an air fill.

USE A DRY FILL HOSE

Everyone knows that water in a scuba cylinder is bad news, but the big question is how does it get there? One would think that the pressure would prevent water from entering the cylinder, so as long as the pressure isn't allowed fall below some nominal level, there would be no problem. Not so. In reality, the most likely place to get water in the cylinder is right at your dive center during an air fill.

Most dive centers place your cylinder in a water tank during the fill process, ostensibly to keep it cooler (nice try) and contain the shrapnel in the event of a cylinder explosion (guess again). Invariably, the fill connector ends up getting wet, and when an untrained or careless technician hooks it up to your cylinder, water droplets are trapped in the space between the fill connector and the cylinder inlet. When the air is turned on, the water is forced into your cylinder. The cumulative effect of a few such fills can be a significant amount of water in your cylinder. So to make sure you get a dry fill, make sure the technician blows some air out of the fill hose and dries off both the fill fitting and the cylinder inlet before hooking up.

5 WATCH WHERE YOU FILL

Using a dry fill hose is only one minor precaution in the grand scheme of getting safe air fills. More important is the quality of maintenance afforded the compressor. At first glance, it appears there's little to the process of filling a scuba cylinder. The compressor squeezes the air molecules closely together and shoves them tightly into the cylinder. We assume the quality of the air inside the cylinder is pretty much the same as the air around us. Nothing could be further from the truth.

In reality, the process of compressing air is wrought with potential problems. First, the compressor draws its inlet air from a specific location. If exhaust fumes from a nearby vehicle, refrigerants from a leaky refrigerator compressor, carbon dioxide and carbon monoxide from gas appliances, fumes from solvents in a maintenance shop or paint facility, or any contaminants from any unknown source drift by the inlet, these contaminants can enter the system. Unless the system has the proper filters, and these filters have been serviced regularly, the contaminants can end up in your cylinder.

Next, the compressor itself may not be clean, and the internal working of the compressor can contaminate the air entering it. Remember that as the air is compressed, it gets hot ñ so hot in fact that some contaminants may even break down, oxidize or combust. Lubricants used to keep the compressor's innards moving smoothly can break down from the heat, and the resulting byproducts end up in the finished product.

Finally we must consider the storage cylinders or air bank filled by the compressor, and used to fill your cylinder. Unless these are free of contaminants, your air may be suspect.

When choosing an air station to get a fill, look for a professionally maintained facility that provides lots of air fills to a number of operators. A center that relies on air fills to stay in business is more likely to pay attention to the details and monitor the quality of its air. Certification by a "name brand" agency such as PADI, NAUI, SSI, IANTD or any of the major dive certification agencies is a sign (but not a guarantee) that the fill station is up to standards.

6 CHECK THE RECORDS

Most reputable dive centers follow a regimen of periodic testing to ensure that their compressor is functioning properly and that the compressed air produced is free of contamination. This may be done quarterly, monthly, or at some other interval. When getting a fill at an unfamiliar dive center, ask to see the results of their most recent air quality test. If they don't have one or won't let you see it, go elsewhere. Remember too that just because the air produced was good last month, last week, or even yesterday is no guarantee that it's good today.

TEST FOR CARBON MONOXIDE

Okay, so now you're suspicious, and you don't want anybody except your own mother filling your cylinder. After all we've just said, it appears there's no way to be sure the air is safe. While this is true to an extent, there is at least one test we can do to check the quality of an air fill. That's a test for carbon monoxide.

Carbon monoxide (CO) is a colorless, odorless gas that is extremely toxic even in very low concentrations. Carbon monoxide binds to the oxygen-carrying sites of red blood cells with a much higher affinity than oxygen. The result is that CO ties up the red blood cells, and prevents the blood from carrying oxygen to our tissues and brain.

Carbon monoxide forms as a result of incomplete combustion. If a compressor overheats or suffers an internal failure, the result may be compressed air laced with lethal levels of CO. One short dive might be all that's needed to fall victim to CO's fatal effects.

Few fatalities are attributed to CO poisoning, but the problem may be more widespread than thought. Several symptoms of CO poisoning are easily confused with other maladies, including seasickness, DCS, and the flu. Headaches, tingling, nausea, and vomiting are all symptoms of CO poisoning, and exposure to CO can severely impair a diver's thought process and judgment.

The standards for grade E compressed air (including breathing air for scuba) limit CO to 10 parts per million (ppm), but the testing laboratories that check air quality for air fill stations routinely find CO levels in excess of this limit in the samples sent for testing. As many as 5 to 10 percent of the monthly samples sent by dive centers participating in air quality monitoring show levels in the 10 to 20 ppm range, with some even reaching the 100 to 200 ppm range.

Fortunately, several manufacturers produce monitors that can test the air in our cylinders for carbon monoxide. Sold under such trade names as Air Guard, Air Check, and C-O-Cop, these devices typically use a colorometric gel sensing technology (color change) to indicate the presence of CO in excessive concentration. The devices are simple to use, reliable, and relatively inexpensive to purchase ($60 to $100 and up). The expendable sensing elements run in the $3 to $6 dollar range per test. For more information, check your local dive center.

8 VERIFY NITROX FILLS

Those who dive with nitrox (air enriched with oxygen) have even more to worry about. The dive times and depths to which dives can safely be made on nitrox are predicated on the oxygen content of the mixture. Too many divers rely on the dive center, a buddy, or good luck to ensure their cylinder contains the percentage of oxygen on which their dive plan is based. If the oxygen level is too low, the diver runs a high risk of decompression sickness. If it's too high, there's a potential for oxygen toxicity. The prospects of either problem should be enough to convince divers to spend the time or money to verify the oxygen content of their nitrox fills.

9 STORE CYLINDERS PROPERLY

Surprisingly, the way we store our cylinders can have a direct impact on the quality of the air inside. To maximize safety, we should store cylinders upright (especially aluminum cylinders) in a cool, dry location with minimal air pressure (50 to 100 psi). Here's why.

Both steel and aluminum cylinders are subject to corrosion, or oxidation. When water is present, the oxygen in the cylinder reacts to form rust (in the case of steel cylinders) or aluminum oxide (aluminum cylinders). The result is a depletion of oxygen in the cylinder, and degradation of the structural integrity of the cylinder. The reaction proceeds at a much faster rate under conditions of high pressure and temperature. By storing the cylinder upright, we present a smaller and stronger area on which the reaction can take place.

If you haven't used your cylinder for several months or years, take it to a reputable dive center for a visual inspection and quality air fill. If you decide to dive with a cylinder that's been laying around for a few months, you really don't know what you'll be breathing.

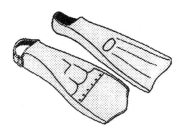

CHAPTER TEN

Ten Tips
to Dodge the
DCS Bullet

1) **Observe the Limits**

2) **Avoid Problem Profiles**

3) **Make Safety Stops**

4) **Use Computer Smarts**

5) **Minimize Cold Exposure**

6) **Avoid Overexertion**

7) **Avoid Alcohol**

8) **Drink Plenty of Fluids**

9) **Avoid Deep and Multi-Day Dives**

10) **Avoid Flying after Diving**

Diving is an adventure, and with all adventure comes an element of risk. As part of our training as divers, we learn to deal with everything from hazardous marine life, to environmental conditions, to equipment problems. Most of us like to think that our training, knowledge and skill will prevent us from any underwater mishap. The real key to success in any adventure is to manage the risk, to minimize our exposure to the hazards. Whether we're talking about sharks, a freeflowing regulator, or high surf and currents, we must first understand what the risks really are, and the factors that contribute to the hazards. Perhaps one of the most important and poorly understood risks in recreational diving is decompression sickness (DCS), and managing the risk of DCS involves a number of factors.

Decompression sickness is not unique to divers. The problem was recognized the 1800's when construction workers in pressurized enclosures called "caissons" built bridge foundations and other structures underwater. These workers would experience sharp pains in the joints after emerging from the caissons, and would often walk in a bent-over posture.

Researchers of the time determined that the cause of the problem, referred to as "caisson's disease" or "the bends," was an accumulation of nitrogen in the body's tissues. As all divers are taught, if we accumulate nitrogen in our system by breathing it at elevated pressure, we must also find a way to safely rid ourselves of the excess. DCS occurs when excess nitrogen evolves in the gaseous form in the body's tissues and blood. The symptoms include joint pain, paralysis, skin irritation and rash, numbness, tingling, fatigue, and a general ill feeling. In some cases, the damage may be irreparable, and even life threatening.

In the early 1900's, Scottish physiologist John Scott Haldane set out to study the problem of decompression and develop a means of avoiding DCS in Royal Navy divers. His work became the foundation for modern decompression theory, and resulted in the first dive tables.

Over the years, the diving community has struggled with its understanding of decompression sickness, and attempted to find ways of reducing the risk of contracting this malady. We know a lot more than we did thirty years ago, but our understanding of the mechanisms by which nitrogen is absorbed and eliminated by the body is far from complete, and the models used to predict and prevent DCS are far from perfect. The only way to avoid DCS completely is to forego diving altogether. Still, for those of us who spit in the eye of the devil and continue to dive, a number of strategies have emerged which can help us dodge the DCS bullet.

1 OBSERVE THE LIMITS

The most obvious strategy for avoiding DCS is to observe the no-decompression limits (NDL's) for recreational diving. Ever since the days of Haldane, scientists and researchers have made steps towards a better understanding of decompression theory, and have developed better models to predict and prevent DCS. In the past two decades, several new tables have emerged based on the new theories and improved models.

Today recreational divers can choose from a variety of dive tables. These include the U.S. Navy tables and variants thereof, the PADI Recreational Dive Planner, and the DCIEM (Canada's Defense and Civil Institute of Environmental Medicine) tables, to mention a few. While the various tables are similar, there are distinct differences. Based on variations in the assumptions and mathematical models used to develop these tables, different tables may prescribe different NDL's, ascent rates, and surface intervals for the same dive profile. No single table is necessarily "better" or "safer" than the others under all circumstances. The important thing is that we know how to use the tables properly, and observe any restrictions they impose upon us.

Especially when diving clear warm waters, we can easily be tempted to dive right to the limits prescribed by our dive tables. Doing so is akin to rushing to the edge of a cliff on a dark, foggy night. Too many of the factors that contribute to the development of DCS symptoms are simply not fully understood. We don't know exactly where that cliff is, and even when we do follow the tables, we can sometimes develop symptoms. To reduce the risk of DCS, we simply put some margin between our bottom time and the NDL, reduce our ascent rate, and extend our surface interval beyond the minimum required for a repetitive dive.

2 AVOID PROBLEM PROFILES

Depth and time aren't the only factors involved in DCS. For years, experts have discouraged divers from particular dive profiles considered more dangerous than others. One such profile is the sawtooth profile—a profile that takes a diver through rising and falling depth excursions throughout the course of a dive. Another problematic dive profile is a reverse profile, that is, a deep dive following a shallow dive. A bounce dive—a rapid dive to a deep depth followed by an immediate return to the surface – is also considered risky. All of these profiles involve physiological changes and processes beyond those upon which the decompression models are based. If you follow one of these profiles, consider yourself a test case. The first dive should be the deepest dive of the day. The first part of the dive should be the deepest part of the dive. Ups and downs during a dive should be minimized as much as practical, and bounce dives should be avoided all together.

3 MAKE SAFETY STOPS

One of the more important changes in dive safety results from a change in philosophy regarding the ascent at the end of a dive. For years, divers were taught to measure bottom time as the elapsed time from initial descent to the beginning of the final ascent, and after reaching the NDL, the rule was to make an immediate 60-foot per minute ascent all the way to the surface. Some divers with an elementary understanding of decompression theory reasoned that spending time in shallow water at the end of the dive would allow them to off-gas more slowly and safely, thus reducing the potential for a DCS "hit" on the surface. Instead of ascending directly to the surface at the end of a dive, these divers would often spend the last few minutes of their dive bubbling around at shallow depth looking for sand dollars, urchin shells, and lobsters.

More recently, scientific studies have borne out the fact that a brief pause in the ascent can reduce the formation of "silent bubbles" (asymptomatic or non-problem bubbles) which many experts believe are a precursor to DCS. Today, the concept has been adopted by recreational diving in the form of a safety stop 6 a brief (three to five minute) stop in the 10 to 20-foot depth range. While a safety stop is a good idea on any dive, it is especially important following dives to depths in excess of 60 feet, or any time we dive to within three to five minutes of our NDL. Don't limit your safety stop to the suggested three to five minutes, either. A longer safety stop does nothing but help avoid DCS.

4. USE COMPUTER SMARTS

Dive computers can be great tools for reducing DCS risk. Designed to constantly monitor depth and bottom, these electronic marvels continuously calculate the theoretical nitrogen uptake and offgassing for various tissue models. The advantage of the computer is that it doesn't miss a move. Since it continuously checks depth and time, it can give us "credit" for the time spent at shallow depths, thus allowing longer dives. Dive computers also measure surface intervals, and provide important planning functions for repetitive dives.

The one thing a dive computer can't do is think for us. In some cases, computers can lull us into a false sense of security. A computer will happily calculate gas absorption and desorption while we follow a sawtooth or reverse dive profile, and may tell us we're within prescribed limits when in fact, we're courting disaster. Just because we have a computer doesn't mean we can forget the basic tenets of safe diving. The computer is merely a tool that helps us make decisions. It should never be allowed to make decisions for us.

 MINIMIZE COLD EXPOSURE

No studies conclusively link cold exposure to DCS, but many experts believe that cold can be a contributing factor in the development of DCS symptoms. After all, cold exposure causes a marked change in a diver's circulation, which obviously affects the uptake and release of nitrogen in the various tissues of a diver's body.

As a precaution, divers should always be conservative with respect to their exposure protection, erring on the side of too warm versus too cold. When diving in cold water, cut the dive short of the published no-decompression limits. Many divers add an extra ten feet to their actual depth when calculating NDL's for cold water dives.

6 AVOID OVEREXERTION

Excessive exertion before, during, or immediately following a dive can alter our circulation, thus affecting nitrogen uptake and offgassing. This can cause our physiology to differ drastically from that on which decompression models are based.

Many dive charters, especially those in resort areas, actually help divers avoid overexertion in the name of customer service. It's not unusual for the boat's crew to load tanks, set up gear, and help divers into and out of the water, thus reducing the stress and strain. To the extent possible, divers should avoid strenuous activities before, during and after a dive. Drift dives, and leisurely boat dives along reefs where little current exists promote low-effort diving.

7 AVOID ALCOHOL

By now you're probably getting the idea that anything which alters our circulation is something to avoid when diving. Alcohol not only affects our circulation, but it can alter the physics and physiology that determines how nitrogen enters and leaves the tissues.

Alcohol is bad news all the way around. First, alcohol changes our circulation, increasing the blood flow to the skin and extremities. It also alters the chemistry of the blood, reducing the surface tension that may cause silent bubbles to grow into "trouble bubbles" Alcohol is a diuretic, meaning that it causes us to urinate more frequently, thus contributing to dehydration. Finally, alcohol affects our central nervous system such that it impairs our ability to make sound judgments. Divers should abstain from alcohol before, during, and for a "reasonable" period after diving.

 ## DRINK PLENTY OF FLUIDS

Dehydration is also a problem for our circulatory system, and is considered a major risk factor for DCS. As we dehydrate, our blood thickens and circulation is impeded. This means nitrogen is less efficiently removed from tissues. The reduced circulation to some areas may mean that inadequate oxygenation of tissues may occur. This all spells trouble since dive tables don't take these factors into account.

Unfortunately, many factors in diving promote dehydration, at least to some extent. Many divers reduce fluid intake prior to diving to avoid the need to relieve themselves on the dive boat or in the water. Diving also causes an immersion response that results in excessive urine production. To make matters worse, the air we breathe while diving is extremely dry, causing us to loose a significant amount of moisture from the lungs.

Dehydration is difficult to detect but easy to prevent. Thirst is a poor indicator of our state of hydration. A better indication is the color of our urine, which in a well-hydrated individual will be nearly clear. To avoid dehydration, avoid drinks with

caffeine or sweeteners. Caffeine is a diuretic, and sugar inter-
feres with the absorption of water. Unsweetened juices are
better, and water is best. Drink about eight ounces every hour.

9 AVOID DEEP AND MULTI-DAY DIVES

Ouch! This one might hurt a bit, but the fact is that the inci-
dence of DCS is higher for those who dive deeper than 80 feet.
There is also a greater risk of DCS for those who make repetitive dives over multiple days. The bottom line is that our
decompression models have a more difficult time accurately
predicting DCS for deep dives and multi-day repetitive dives.
Although factors such as dehydration, fatigue, and overexertion
may be the real culprits, nobody knows for certain. However,
the numbers don't lie. If you're serious about reducing your risk,
stay away from deep and multi-day repetitive dives.

10 AVOID FLYING AFTER DIVING

One unfortunate reality is that getting to a dive destination
often involves flying, and at the end of the dive vacation, the
desire for diving may collide with the risk factor of altitude
exposure in an aircraft.

Remember that the dive tables are designed to allow us to
ascend to the surface (assumed to be at the standard sea level

pressure) with minimal risk of DCS. Airliners usually maintain a cabin pressure roughly equivalent to an altitude of 5,000 to 8,000 feet above sea level. While we may be fine on the surface following a dive, an ascent to a higher altitude in an aircraft (or walking or driving for that matter) puts us at a lower ambient pressure that may induce DCS. (See the sidebar on Flying after Diving)

The complexities of decompression sickness may never be completely understood, and there will probably never be a dive table or computer that guarantees complete safety from DCS. Still, armed with a basic knowledge of the contributing factors and by following published safe diving procedures, we can manage the risk while still enjoying the beauty, freedom, and adventure offered by the sport.

Flying After Diving

In recent years, the problem of DCS associated with flying after diving has received much attention. Unfortunately, nobody knows how many divers fly after diving, or how soon after diving they fly, so it's impossible to derive a quantitative statistical basis for flying after diving guidelines. However, the known cases of DCS associated with flying after diving speak for themselves. Of the divers who report DCS symptoms when flying, almost all occurred within 24 hours of diving. This in itself suggests divers wait 24 hours before flying. However, many of the cases involved multi-day repetitive dives, as well as other potential factors that muddy the water. While there is no way to

completely eliminate the possibility of DCS when flying after diving, the current guidelines are as follows:

✓ Divers who make only one no-decompression dive
per day should wait 12 hours before ascending to

altitude in an aircraft, automobile, or by any other
means.

✓ Divers who make decompression dives or repetitive
dives, especially over multiple days, should wait 24
hours before ascending to altitude.

✓ Experts agree that taking a day off from diving in the
middle of an extended dive vacation can help reduce
the risk of DCS. Another good strategy for reducing
the risk is to avoid diving the day before you fly home
(or drive to altitude) from a diving vacation.